FEARLESS

Free in Christ in an Age of Anxiety

FEARLESS

Free in Christ in an Age of Anxiety

by RACHEL STARR THOMSON
CAROLYN CURREY
MERCY HOPE

1:11 Publishing

Fearless: Free in Christ in an Age of Anxiety

Published by 1:11 Publishing
An imprint of Little Dozen Press
Crystal Beach, ON, Canada
littledozen.com

ISBN: 978-1-927658-45-1

"Fear is a reaction. Courage is a decision."
—WINSTON S. CHURCHILL

"Fear not, for I am with you;
be not dismayed, for I am your God.
I will strengthen you, yes, I will help you,
I will uphold you with My righteous right hand."
—ISAIAH 41:10

TABLE OF CONTENTS

1
Chapter

POWER, LOVE, AND A SOUND MIND

Shortly before he was crucified, Jesus told the story of the parable of the talents. The story goes like this: a rich man called three of his servants together just before he went away on a journey and entrusted parts of his fortune to them. He gave one servant five "talents" (a talent was a unit of money), one servant two, and the final servant one, "to each according to his own ability" (Matthew 25:14-30).

The rich man went on his journey, and the three servants went to work with their gifts—well, two of them did. "After a long time" the master returned to settle accounts.

The first servant proudly told the master that he had invested his five talents and produced five more. The gift given to him had multiplied. "Well done, good and faithful servant!" the master declared. "You were faithful over a few things; I will put you in charge of many things. Share your master's joy!"

The second servant likewise presented his results: he too had doubled his money. He received exactly the same reward from the master.

Finally the third servant came forward. This time the scene was different. Rather than mutual joy and excitement over multiplication and fruitfulness, this servant says, "Master, I know you. You're a difficult man, reaping where you haven't sown and gathering where you haven't scattered seed. *So I was afraid and went off and hid your talent in the ground.* Look, you have what is yours."

The master's response is harsh. Rather than being sympathetic toward the man's fear, he calls him "You evil, lazy servant," and says that at the very least, he should have put the money in a bank so it would gather interest.

He then instructs that the one talent be taken away from this servant and given to the one who has ten. The servant himself is thrown out of the master's service.

This is a familiar story, and for many of us the reaction is the same. Something inside us says, "Not fair!"

This man was only given one talent. He wasn't equipped. He got shorted from the start. Maybe his fears were justified; the master was harsh and unreasonable.

But There's a Twist

This story isn't all it seems to be on the surface. Its ancient hearers would have heard it correctly, but we're a little deafened by the word "talent."

In its original context, this word was a unit of measurement, specifically of weight. A "talent" was like a pound or a ton. Since money in the ancient world had its value measured by substance (gold, silver) and weight, a talent was a certain amount of money.

A pretty big amount.

How big? Just how much money are we talking? When we read this story through modern eyes we're tempted to think the last servant got the equivalent of ten bucks. No wonder he buried it; that kind of money can be lost in a matter of minutes. With so little to work with, he only had one chance to get it right. That kind of scarcity can be paralyzing!

Most of us probably identify more with the one-talent guy than the other two servants. Compared to others, we don't feel like we have much to offer. We're afraid of losing the little we do have. We may feel like the world (or even God) is against us.

The man with only one talent buried it out of fear. We tend to feel like that wasn't such a bad call.

But we don't quite read the numbers correctly. A talent wasn't equivalent to ten bucks, or twenty, or even a hundred. What the man was given equaled *fifty years' wages*—in today's dollars, roughly $1.25 million dollars.

You Have a Gift, and It Is Immensely Valuable

The point of Jesus's parable isn't that God has given each of us an enormous sum of money. Obviously that's not true. He's using money as a picture of something else—the gifts God has given and entrusted to every person.

This is actually how "talent" came to have its current meaning in English—that of a gift or an innate skill that someone is born with. Even today we tend to describe such gifts as "God-given."

Several key points stand out in this story, and we want you to see them clearly:

1 Every person—including you—has been given a gift by God.

2 Every gift is of immense value, no matter how it might compare to someone else's gifts. No one got a cheap or valueless gift from God.

3 Every gift has the capacity to multiply (and is meant to do so).

4 The gifts are essentially "on loan," meant to be stewarded.

To recap: You have been given something of immense value. You have also been given the ability to multiply it. Even if you have received the least of all possible gifts, it is still the spiritual equivalent of a million dollars!

First Corinthians 12:4-11 tells us the same thing in plain language: "Now there are different gifts, but the same Spirit. There are different ministries, but the same Lord. And there are different activities, but the same God activates each gift in each person . . . One and the same Spirit is active in all these, distributing to each person as He wills."

We should notice a couple of other things as well. The gifts in the parable were given "according to each one's ability." God knew exactly what each person was equipped to handle and to handle *well*. The third servant didn't lack ability to make good use of the gift given to him.

Finally, the master did not return until "after a long time." The servant had all the time, money, and ability to do something great with what he was given, but he chose not to use any of it. He feared risk so much that his fears became a self-fulfilling prophecy. Given an enormous gift he was afraid to lose, he ended up with nothing.

The Thief in the Background

The servant in the parable got robbed. Because of his master's generosity, he was made quite rich—but a thief stole everything he had and then some.

The thief was *fear*.

Why, in a book about fear, are we making such a big deal out of the principle that you have been given something of immense value?

Because fear is more than a feeling, and the consequences of being controlled by fear are bigger than you are. The Bible uses many pictures to describe our lives in this world, and fear will make you ineffective in every single one of them.

- If life is a battle, fear will keep you off the front lines.

- If life is a race, fear will stop you from running it.

- If life is a wrestling match, fear will prevent you from getting in the ring.

- If life is an opportunity, fear will stop you from investing.

Life is full of real risks. In one sense, there are lots of good reasons to be afraid. Victory requires a fight. But the greatest risk of all is that you *won't* fight—that you'll allow fear to keep you on the couch, with your talent buried in the ground and all of its multiplying effects dormant and dead.

If you get up to fight a battle, you might lose. But if you choose never to fight, the loss is guaranteed.

Freedom from Feelings?

The legendary World War II general George S. Patton once said, "All men are afraid in battle. The coward is the one who lets his fear overcome his sense of duty."

Irrational fears exist. They range from extreme phobias (of things as varied as the outdoors, insects, and the number thirteen) to common irrational fears like the anxiety many of us feel in the dark. But there are also rational fears—good reasons to be afraid. How do we deal with these?

In this book, we're going to talk about living free from fear. But we aren't proposing that you can (or should) live free from feelings. "Fear" is something of a catch-all term in English, so we want to break it down here and make it clear what we're talking about.

At its most basic, fear is a feeling or instinct given to us for our own protection. For example, most of us would feel fear if asked to jump off a skyscraper or wrestle an alligator. We might feel instinctively afraid of a stranger in a dark alley or of walking across thin ice.

This kind of fear, just a feeling that tells you there is danger ahead, isn't bad. Fear becomes a bad thing, a thief and an enemy, when the good instinct goes too far. It doesn't discriminate well between what really is harmful and what is just "scary" because it's outside of our comfort zone. It predicts the future for us and tells us what we "can't do." It starts to run roughshod in our thought lives and in our emotions. And so it begins to direct our lives.

When fear gets the reins of our lives, it becomes what we might call cowardice. We don't like to think of ourselves as cowards, but the temptation to cowardice is very strong, and when we give in, this type of fear will displace God and control our lives. This is just as true for Christians as for anyone else!

This "bad fear" is the good natural instinct given to us by God after it has morphed into a monster. It is a helpful instinct blown out of all proportion, applied indiscriminately and often irrationally. It particularly becomes a problem when it stops us from walking out the call of God in our lives—whether that means obeying God by moving to Africa or just obeying him by loving the neighbor down the street.

So in this book, we aren't talking about getting free from *feelings* of anxiety, stress, or worry (even though one side effect of living free from fear is that those feelings can and will lessen). We are talking about getting free of cowardice: getting out of the grip and control of fear as a guiding force in our lives and putting God in the first place where he deserves to be.

Do It Afraid

In her book *Do It Afraid: Obeying God in the Face of Fear,* Joyce Meyer writes, "Just because you feel fear doesn't mean you can't do it. Do it afraid."

Carolyn's Story: Over my years as a dancer I've had my share of injuries, but none so dramatic as the five times my kneecap dislocated. The first time this happened I was about fourteen, and recovering from that injury was a real mental hurdle. As I began the daily routine of class again, I faced fear even when standing on the leg that had suffered the injury. Landing a jump on that leg or turning on it was terrifying because the possibility of a recurring injury was always there.

At that point I had to make a choice. Would I shut down and stop dancing because I was afraid, or would I keep dancing, face the fear, and get stronger?

I ended up choosing a middle road. I kept dancing and learned to do it (mostly) without fear. But whenever I had a choice, I unconsciously used the uninjured leg to support me, and it became the stronger leg. This also caused muscles in the other leg to tighten and loosen in such a way that would cause the injury to recur, which it did four more times before I finally realized what was going on. Once again I had to face fear and consciously train that leg to be used equally for support. It wasn't until I faced my fear in full that I began dancing in true strength.

Timothy was a young man in the first century AD who became one of the earliest leaders among Jesus's followers in the Gentile world. The apostle Paul met him while traveling through the Greek world on a missionary journey, and he took Timothy along with him. He mentored Timothy and eventually entrusted him with authority as a teacher and elder in these young churches.

The demands on Timothy in this situation were intense. Christianity was a very new and very young faith, still developing its core beliefs and practices. It was often a target for persecution from local governments and other religious groups, both pagan and Jewish. Timothy himself was half-Jewish and half-Gentile, and because of this he was controversial and a natural target for those who wanted to divide the church along ethnic lines. Paul, Timothy's mentor and close friend, was essentially a magnet for persecution and controversy himself. Timothy inherited all of this.

On top of that, Timothy and Paul traveled extensively in a world before airplanes, massive ships, and highway systems cushioned us from the effects of nature. They experienced shipwreck, risked attack from bandits or wild animals, and dealt with the ever-present threats of bad weather, bad roads, hunger, thirst, and disease.

There was a lot in Timothy's world, in other words, to be afraid of.

But Timothy also had gifts. Paul (and God) had entrusted him with spiritual gifts of understanding, scriptural knowledge, leadership in the church, and more. We aren't told exactly what gifts Paul imparted to Timothy, but we are told that he did. Like you and me, Timothy had an immensely valuable contribution to make.

The question was, would he make it? Or would he allow fear to rob him of his purpose—and the world of its results?

This is the context of a familiar verse that will become our keystone in this book. In 2 Timothy 1:6 Paul writes to his protege, "Therefore, I remind you to keep ablaze the gift of God that is in you through the laying on of my hands." In the next verse, the keystone verse, Paul highlights both the *threat* to Timothy's gift and the path to *overcoming* that threat: "For God has not given us a spirit of fear, but of power and of love and of a sound mind" (2 Timothy 1:7).

Throughout this book, we will be unpacking that verse in greater depth.

Choosing to Be Free

The power and pressure fear exerts on us can be enormous. What 1 John 4:18 plainly tells us is true: fear has torment. In our culture, more and more people are turning to drugs to help them manage anxiety and fear. But there is a better way.

Although it may not always feel like it, living free from fear is a choice. No one expects you to snap your fingers and be loosed from anxiety (remember, this isn't about freedom from feelings), but you can make choices that move you toward a life free from both the control and the torment of fear.

If you feel like you can't possibly overcome your fears on your own . . . you don't have to! God gives us choices, but he also promises to empower our choices when we walk in obedience to him.

Paul didn't tell Timothy that he could keep his gifts ablaze just by his own willpower. Rather, he said it was possible because God would give three gifts that would empower Timothy to overcome fear. These three gifts are power, love, and a sound mind. The word used for "fear" in this passage highlights the idea of timidity or cowardice. The fear that torments and keeps us locked in self-fulfilling prophecy and self-destructive life patterns can be broken.

Never underestimate the power of choice. In general, people want to attribute success in life to absolutely everything except choice. We want to say someone did great things because they were lucky, or they were beautiful, or they had a better job, or they had great parents, or they were born in the right place, or they're uniquely gifted. All those things are blessings that can definitely benefit the one who has them—but remember, we have *all* been given gifts, and no matter how our gifts and talents stack up against someone else's, they are immensely valuable in their own right.

> NEVER UNDERESTIMATE THE POWER OF CHOICE.
>
> SUCCESS IS THE RESULT OF CHOICES, EMPOWERED BY GOD'S BLESSING.

When it comes down to it, success is the result of choices, empowered by God's blessing.

So as we journey together through this book, we want to encourage you to make some choices.

Choose to be open. Choose to learn. Choose to practice what you learn, to activate the insights God gives you as we study his Scriptures together. Choose to embrace the process, though at times the process may be messy.

Above all, choose to risk.

God has given you the gifts, the time, and the ability to use what he has given.

The only way you can lose is by never trying at all.

Are you ready? Let's go.

2
Chapter

FEAR OF THE LORD

When we say that you can live fearless, what comes to mind?

There's a good chance you picture a daredevil, an adrenaline junkie scaling cliffs or jumping off skyscrapers with the slogan "YOLO" emblazoned on his back. Our culture equates fearlessness with recklessness.

It should be clear by now that we don't share this definition. While we salute those who greet life with zeal and are willing to take risks, the world's view of fearlessness too often tilts toward a self-destructive way of being that ironically is often driven by fear—of relationship, intimacy, boredom, or the need to honestly confront oneself.

Remember that the Bible equates living free of the "spirit of fear" with operating in love, power, and a sound mind. Self-destructive behaviors do not include any of these things.

Rather, the kind of fearlessness we are talking about is freedom from the control and dominance of fear. We'll talk about this more in the next chapter, but to sum it up here: Fear is not neutral. It's not harmless. It's not just a feeling. Fear actually seeks control over your life.

Fear and God are competing for the same place in your life. They both want lordship.

So how do we make sure fear doesn't get the throne? How do we make sure that fear doesn't win?

It's counterintuitive, but the best way to make sure fear does not rule our lives is to cultivate a special kind of fear. What the Bible calls "the fear of God" is the highest form of natural fear. It is the one truly appropriate and healthy fear. And it is what sets you free from fear of anything and everything else.

The Fear that Is Love

We first meet Joshua in the book of Exodus, where he is called Moses's assistant (Exodus 24:13). One of his key jobs was acting as commander of the Israelite army (Exodus 17), but we also see him accompanying Moses into the presence of God and following him around everywhere. Whether Joshua knew it or not, he was being groomed to take Moses's place as leader of the nomadic nation of Israel, and he was the one God would appoint to lead the people into the land of Canaan to wage war against its inhabitants and claim their inheritance.

Israel's wilderness era was a time when they regularly and dramatically encountered the presence of God. God's presence could be terrifying. When God came down on Mount Sinai, Scripture tells us there was "thick darkness," lightning, the sound of trumpets, and earthquakes. On more than one occasion, when Israel sinned, the presence of God broke out in the form of a consuming fire that brought destruction within the camp. Israel knew God as the One who had delivered them from Egypt in a staggering display of power over life and death, and as the One who demanded holiness ("set-apartness") and obedience from his people.

This lifestyle of close encounters with the presence of God provoked two very different reactions from the people. Interestingly, we would call both reactions "fear."

Early on, the nation as a whole rejected God's invitation to purify themselves and come into his presence. They wanted Moses to go into God's presence for them, both hearing from and speaking to God on their behalf. Over time they made it evident that their "fear of God" was rooted in distrust and unbelief. When they encountered difficulties on their desert journey, they often accused God of trying to kill them, and more than once they nearly jumped ship altogether, threatening to overthrow Moses, appoint a new leader, and return to Egypt, where they had been slaves and the target of genocidal policies, rather than continue to walk with God.

Joshua's response was very different. In Exodus 33, we read that when Moses would go into the tent of meeting to meet with God and speak to him "face to face, just as a man speaks with his friend," Joshua would accompany him. Then, even after Moses had left, Joshua continued to linger inside the tent. He hungered for the presence of God.

Joshua loved, honored, and respected God more than anything or anyone else. He trembled at God's presence, reverencing him and treating him with awe. He understood that God was jealous for Israel in the same way a husband is jealous for his wife, desiring Israel's full loyalty and love.

While the rest of Israel refused to encounter God any more than necessary, Joshua actively sought God's presence. *Their fear of God was cowardice; his was love.*

Godly Fear

In the last chapter we talked about fear as a natural, God-given instinct meant to protect us and draw appropriate boundaries around our lives. But like so many other instincts, fear applied in the wrong ways and to the wrong things becomes crippling. It becomes a thief and an enemy.

Scripture uses two different Hebrew words for "fear." One of these connotes reverence or awe. The other connotes alarm or terror. Both are applied to "fear of the Lord."

If "bad fear" is our natural instinct gone amuck, "godly fear" is our natural instinct in its highest form.

> IF "BAD FEAR" IS OUR NATURAL INSTINCT GONE AMUCK, "GODLY FEAR" IS OUR NATURAL INSTINCT IN ITS HIGHEST FORM.

its highest form. Joshua walked in the fear of the Lord. The Israelites were controlled by "bad fear," the natural instinct of fear applied where it should not have been. They were unbelieving and doubtful toward God and therefore were afraid of every challenging circumstance and obstacle they encountered, whether it was giants in the land, starvation in the wilderness, or even fear of God's presence.

Godly fear, by contrast, goes hand in hand with love. We can see this dynamic at work anytime we love something that is in some sense greater, wilder, or more powerful than we are. People who love the wilderness, for example, also fear it. People who love the ocean have a healthy fear of its power. People who most genuinely love other people also "fear" them—they recognize their uniqueness and separateness from themselves and revere that, respecting the one they love rather than seeking to control them. When we love people, we recognize that they are not tools to be used for our own self-gratification, but they are to be honored for who they are.

In the same way, people who love God most also tremble in his presence. There is literally a weight and a fire to the presence and glory of God, and it is terrifying—but in a way that makes us more alive.

This kind of fear sets boundaries around our lives. But by doing so it also sets us free.

This is what the God-given instinct of *fear* is meant to be. It is the opposite of the low, perverted form of fear we battle, the ungodly fear that seeks to cripple our lives and keep us subservient to lesser gods.

Unpacking the Fear of the Lord

It can be challenging for us to think about a kind of fear that goes hand-in-hand with love, but that is what the Bible means when it talks about fear of the Lord. Fear of the Lord reverences and honors God for who he is actually is. This means recognizing how great, wild, and "other" he is: he isn't us, he isn't human, he could snuff us all out with a thought. But it also means recognizing and revering his character as he has revealed it: he is faithful, he is compassionate, he is the Giver of life.

This double-sided coin explains why the Bible so consistently links *fearing God* to loving and trusting him.

> "And now, Israel, what does the LORD your God require of you, but to *fear the LORD your God, to walk in all his ways, and to love him, to serve the LORD your God with all your heart and with all your soul.*"
> (Deuteronomy 10:12, NKJV)

"Behold, the eye of the LORD is on those *who fear him, on those who hope in his mercy."* (Psalm 33:18)

"You who fear the LORD, trust in the LORD; he is their help and their shield." (Psalm 115:11)

Practically speaking, fearing the Lord means living in total loyalty and devotion to him. We can also call this "holiness," a topic we'll explore more deeply in another chapter.

Fear of the Lord is wholehearted. During a revival in ancient Israel, the king, Jehoshaphat, commanded the priests, "Thus you shall act in the fear of the LORD, faithfully and with a loyal heart" (2 Chronicles 19:9). In many ways, this is the essence of faith. To have faith in God is both to trust him and to be faithful to him. The practical expression of our faith is trust and loyalty.

Thankfully, God doesn't expect faith to develop in a vacuum. He always gives reasons for it: his promises, his actions, the revelation of his character in his Word, his gifts to each one of us (starting with the gift of life!), his behavior in history.

Our choice is to respond to those reasons with faith or with unbelief. God offers us a revelation of himself as trustworthy. It's our choice to believe that or not.

The prophet Samuel encouraged the people of his day, "Only fear the LORD, and serve him in truth with all your heart; *for consider what great things he has done for you*" (1 Samuel 12:24, NKJV). The more that you walk with the Lord, the more you understand that you have reasons for confidence in him. The more you put your confidence in him, understand his holiness, and fear him, the more you will see the pattern of his faithfulness in your life, and the more you will have confidence to put your trust in him. It's a virtuous cycle: an ongoing, relationship-based revelation that produces hope (Romans 5:3-5).

On the other hand, if we choose unbelief and resistance to God, fearing other things more than we fear the Lord, we will tend to interpret everything he does through a lens of unbelief. Like the Israelites, we will develop a belief that God is out to get us, and nothing he does will convince us otherwise.

Giants in the Land

In Numbers 13, we encounter Joshua again. At this point, the people of Israel have been in the desert for about two years. They have received the law and entered a covenantal relationship with Yahweh. Now they have reached the borders of the land God promised them, and it is time to enter and take possession.

At this point Moses chose twelve spies to go and scout out the land, one for each of the twelve tribes of Israel. One of these was Joshua, his assistant.

When the spies returned, they all agreed that God had promised them a good land. "We went into the land where you sent us," they told Moses in the presence of the entire nation. "Indeed it is flowing with milk and honey, and here is some of its fruit."

But that wasn't all they had to say.

"However, the people living in the land are strong, and the cities are large and fortified. We also saw the descendants of Anak [giants] there . . ."

Then Caleb quieted the people in the presence of Moses and said, "We must go up and take possession of the land because we can certainly conquer it!"

But the men who had gone up with him responded, "We can't go up against the people because they are stronger than we are!" So they gave a negative report to the Israelites about the land they had scouted: "The land we passed through to explore is one that devours its inhabitants, and all the people we saw in it are men of great size. We even saw the Nephilim there—the descendants of Anak come from the Nephilim! To ourselves we seemed like grasshoppers, and we must have seemed the same to them." (Numbers 13:27-33)

Other translations call the "negative report" the spies gave "an evil report." *Evil* is an appropriate word. In English, the history of the word "evil" includes the idea of rot or corrosion. The spies' negative, fearful focus on the giants, coupled with their general distrust of God's heart toward them, undermined the confidence of the people. It rotted their resolution and corroded their courage.

The same people whose response to the presence of God was "we don't want to come in close to you; we want to stay at a distance—Moses, you go into God's presence for us" responded to the presence of the giants with fear and refusal to go in and take dominion. They were afraid of God instead of fearing God. As a result, when it came to taking dominion, they responded with cowardice.

Two of the spies, however, responded very differently. We've already seen the response of Caleb above. The other spy whose report did not focus on the giants in the land was Joshua.

It wasn't that Caleb and Joshua didn't see the giants—they did. It was just that they believed God would empower them to overcome. They feared God, and because they feared God, they *believed* him. Their fear went hand in hand with love and trust, and these left no room for fear of the giants, because God had already promised them that they would overcome. Proverbs 14:26 (KJV) describes the state of their hearts: "In the fear of the LORD is strong confidence: and his children shall have a place of refuge."

Their fear of God also elbowed out another common fear: that of other people. They were very much in the minority in this situation. At times, fear of the Lord means standing alone. For many people, a major subconscious fear is the fear of standing apart from the crowd. For whatever reason, we have a very strong herd instinct, and most of us don't like to get out in front or be exceptional in any way. We might call this "fear of man," and it is a direct counter to fear of God. Like other fears, it wants the same throne God does.

Numbers 14 tells the rest of the story:

Then the whole community broke into loud cries, and the people wept that night. All the Israelites complained about Moses and Aaron, and the whole community told them, "If only we had died in the land of Egypt, or if only we had died in this wilderness! Why is the LORD bringing us into this land to die by the sword? Our wives and little children will become plunder. Wouldn't it be better for us to go back to Egypt?" So they said to one another, "Let's appoint a leader and go back to Egypt."

Then Moses and Aaron fell down with their faces to the ground in front of the whole assembly of the Israelite community. Joshua son of Nun and Caleb son of Jephunneh, who were among those who scouted out the land, tore their clothes and said to the entire Israelite community: "The land we passed through and explored is an extremely good land. If the LORD is pleased with us, He will bring us into this land, a land flowing with milk and honey, and give it to us. *Only don't rebel against the LORD, and don't be afraid of the people of the land, for we will devour them. Their protection has been removed from them, and the LORD is with us. Don't be afraid of them!"* (Numbers 14:1-9)

The Israelites responded by threatening to stone their leaders and return to Egypt. Disaster was averted when the glory of the LORD, God's manifest and terrifying presence, suddenly fell on the camp. The result of this episode was that God sentenced the entire generation of Israelites to wander in the wilderness for forty years until they died. They would not enter the land, but their children would. Only Caleb and Joshua would go into the land from their generation.

The Lord Is with Us

Overcoming fear is not about winning a mental or emotional battle. It's not about convincing ourselves that nothing bad could ever happen to us. Instead, fear gets off the throne of our lives when fear of the LORD gets on. Bad fear isn't dissolved in a puddle of positive thinking. It's displaced by trust.

Joshua's logic was simple: Yes, the land is full of giants. Yes, they are powerful and strong. But it doesn't matter. *We will be able to beat them, because the LORD is with us.*

As we saw in the last chapter, we are all given immense value by God, and we are called to put it to work. We are called to step out and take risks as we take dominion and become fruitful in the kingdom of God. Fear will try to stop us from doing this. Fear will point out the giants in the land. It will point out the bad things that could happen and that have happened to other people. It will point out our own smallness and weakness. It will give an evil report.

The evil report won't necessarily be inaccurate. The world is in fact full of dangers. If we risk, we might lose it all. We are small and weak. There are giants in the land.

But fear of God says, "That is all irrelevant. The relevant fact is that God is with you, and you can trust him."

This is the central message of Joshua's entire life. At the end of the book of Deuteronomy, we read about his commissioning as Moses's successor. The words Joshua himself spoke forty years earlier, "The LORD is with us; don't be afraid!" are now spoken back to him. The Lord himself had earlier told Moses, "But commission Joshua *and encourage [i.e. fill with courage] and strengthen him,* for he will cross over ahead of the people and enable them to inherit this land that you will see" (Deuteronomy 3:28).

> Moses then summoned Joshua and said to him in the sight of all Israel, "Be strong and courageous, for you will go with this people into the land the LORD swore to give to their fathers. You will enable them to take

possession of it. *The LORD is the One who will go before you. He will be with you; He will not leave you or forsake you. Do not be afraid or discouraged."* (Deuteronomy 31:7)

At this point the glory of the Lord once again descended, and God spoke to both Moses and Joshua directly. To Joshua he said: *"Be strong and courageous,* for you will bring the Israelites into the land I swore to them, *and I will be with you"* (Deuteronomy 31:23).

After the death of Moses, Yahweh repeated this admonition to Joshua one more time: "I will be with you, just as I was with Moses. I will not leave you or forsake you. Be strong and courageous . . . Haven't I commanded you: be strong and courageous? Do not be afraid or discouraged, for the LORD your God is with you wherever you go" (Joshua 1:5-6, 9).

To Joshua, the promise that Yahweh was with him was not empty words. Joshua had been faithful over a long period of time. He had undergone that "virtuous cycle" we mentioned above, walking with God in a relationship that produced more and more revelation and trust. He had been ready to go into the land as a young man, but he had to wait forty years because of the cowardice of others. Forty years later he still had the same mindset. His readiness to go into the land was not a flash-in-the-pan bravado, because it was based in whole-hearted devotion to Yahweh. He and Caleb had seen Yahweh provide and protect in miraculous ways. They had heard the revelation of God's justice, holiness, and love as given in the law. They took all this to heart.

While the rest of their generation died off because of their fear, Joshua and Caleb grew in faith. They developed a personal history with God. The idea of Yahweh's presence became an idea with substance. For them, "I will be with you" brought to mind years of faithfulness, displays of power, promises, and revelation of God's character.

Through years of worship and actively seeking God's presence, Joshua developed a fear of God that was aligned with the character of God. He feared—reverenced and honored—God. He even knew what the terror of God felt like. He had stood in the presence of fire, trumpets, and earthquakes. He had quaked in his boots at the voice of God. He had literally trembled to see and hear God.

And yet all of this grew his faith. *He feared God in a way that aligned with God's character rather than being afraid of God in a way that did not.*

A Life that Transcends Fear

Shortly after Moses died, the people of Israel crossed the Jordan River and prepared to conduct their first battle for the land. That evening, Joshua looked up and saw a man standing in front of him with a drawn sword in his hand. Joshua approached him and asked whose side he was on—Israel's or their enemies'.

The man responded, "Neither. I have now come as commander of the LORD's army." When Joshua realized he was talking to God himself, he bowed in worship (Joshua 5:13-15).

Think about this story. Joshua saw a man with a drawn sword in his hand. This is the equivalent of seeing someone with a gun cocked and ready and pointed at you. But Joshua's response is incredibly calm. In a situation that for most people would invoke immediate "fight or flight" instincts, he neither attacks the man nor flees. Instead, he *approaches him and asks him a question.* He confronts the man. When he realizes it's the Lord, he falls on his face.

Ninety-nine percent of people would have reacted with fear to the man with the drawn sword; Joshua reacts with fear when he realizes it's the Lord. The moment he understands who he's talking to, he hits the deck and worships. He's not afraid of the drawn sword. Even the fact that he *asks*—doesn't shoot first and ask questions later—shows how unafraid he was. He was set apart and unusual by virtue of his relationship with God.

At this point in Joshua's life, it is obvious that ordinary fear has been almost completely displaced by the fear of the Lord. Joshua is totally uncontrolled by fear, not because he's not aware of the dangers or because he's a mentally strong person, but because he is confident in the character of God and knows that God is with him and on his side. When he was commissioned as leader, Joshua was given the exhortation to "be strong and courageous" three times—once by Moses and twice directly by Yahweh. The rationale for this strength and courage is not Joshua's own ability or a logical breakdown of the facts. He can have courage because Yahweh is with him.

> JOSHUA IS TOTALLY UNCONTROLLED BY FEAR, NOT BECAUSE HE'S NOT AWARE OF THE DANGERS... BUT BECAUSE HE IS CONFIDENT IN THE CHARACTER OF GOD.

We too can live lives that transcend fear. It won't

happen in an instant. As our faith grows and we choose, time after time after time, to trust in the Lord and fear him, "bad fear" will get nudged completely off the throne.

The answer to the problem of fear is counterintuitive indeed: we are set free from fear's control when we grow in the fear of the Lord.

If that seems unattainable, and you can't imagine living with the kind of confident set-apartness that marked the life of Joshua, the message to you is exactly the same as it was to him: Don't be afraid. Be strong and courageous, for the Lord is with you. Start where you are. Choose trust instead of fear in each situation that presents itself. Seek the presence of God. Study his character. Obey him in the little things. Grow in your faith.

Nobody starts with big faith. We all start small. It's the choices we make along the way, the interpretations we choose and the actions we take, that grow our faith or dismantle it.

There were giants in the land when Israel approached its borders, but those giants never defeated them. Their own fear did. Forty years later, when a new generation entered the land in faith and the fear of the Lord, the giants fell.

3
Chapter

FEAR IS REAL ESTATE

It was a gorgeous late winter day on top of a mountain in Northern California. Napa Valley, with its acres of vineyards, stretched out below, the sun filtering through rising wisps of early morning mist—a perfect morning for espresso and good conversation.

"When I was in seminary," our friend said, "I told God there were two things I could never do. I could never be a youth pastor, and I never could serve in the desert. I hated the desert." He laughed. "Of course, I graduated, and what did God do? Called me to serve as a youth pastor in Tucson, Arizona."

He didn't love Tucson. He didn't love youth pastoring. He did it for a couple of years, grew in character, learned a lot, and moved on. "Never tell God never," he said with a chuckle.

It's almost a joke in the church: "Never tell God you'll never do something, because he'll call you to do it." It's right up there with "Never ask God for patience, because he'll make your life miserable." Both adages cast God as having a bit of a twisted streak. But the "never tell God never" stories are common—very common, enough that they can't be coincidental. Almost everyone has one.

So what is God up to here?

That morning as I (Rachel) sipped hot coffee and watched the sun rise over Napa Valley, God showed me what he's up to. It hit all of a sudden, one of those flash revelations that forever changes the way you see something. It really had nothing to do with deserts, or youth pastoring, or learning not to tell God "never," or even learning hard lessons about obedience.

It was about overcoming fear.

In my spirit I heard God whisper, *"If you will build walls around your lives, I will challenge them every time. I love you too much to let you cage yourself in."*

Fear Has Consequences

In the last chapter we saw that Israel's fear had extraordinarily real consequences. When they reached the promised land and saw giants walking around, their fear told them they could not enter the land.

So they couldn't.

Fear might seem like a small thing to us, just a feeling, only human, something we should maybe be coddled over.

Yet fear isn't neutral. It manifests. It may manifest as arbitrary walls we build around our lives—walls that have nothing to do with reality and yet will shape our identity and cage our effectiveness. *I can't work with youth. I can't go overseas. I could never live in a place like that. I could never lead. I'm not cut out for success. I could never learn that skill. I can't ever be loved. I am not enough. I have nothing to offer.*

Or it may manifest, as it did for the Israelites, as blatant unbelief. *No matter how good the land may be, I can't go in. The blessing is a trick. There are giants in the land, and God will not empower me to overcome them. God can't be trusted; he is a liar.*

One thing we can be sure of: if we allow fear to build

walls and make the rules, God will challenge them. He loves us too much to allow us to cripple ourselves. And yet our free will always plays a part. God will challenge your walls, but you have to choose to let them come down. You might have to do it afraid, but do it.

Stolen Lives

Two generations ago Franklin Delano Roosevelt said, "There is nothing to fear but fear itself." It's a profound statement: as we've seen throughout this book, often the real enemy isn't the thing fear says we should be afraid of; *it's the fear itself.*

Fear steals life in all kinds of ways. For example, there's the torment involved in fear, worry, and anxiety. Someone wise on the Internet once said, "Ninety percent of the things you fear will never happen, but worry will make sure that you suffer through every one of them."

Fear also creates self-fulfilling prophecies. It's actually fear of economic collapse that causes economic collapse, as people rush on the banks to pull their money out of play en masse. Fear of violence can lead to violence: think of the tragic rash of killings in the United States where police have fired on unarmed African Americans.

Did those police, in every case, hate black people? Probably not, but there was a level of subconscious fear at play—one that makes a black man reaching for his ID look like he is reaching for a gun. And of course, once a few young black men have learned that white police will fire on them even if they're unarmed, it's not surprising if a few more start carrying guns for protection.

These are complex issues, and we don't mean to oversimplify them—but at the same time, the role of fear is central. Fear leads to self-fulfilling prophecy in the area of violence all the time. It's not uncommon for someone who is afraid of intruders to shoot and kill a family member who comes home late at night. People who are so afraid of disease that they oversanitize their surroundings or overmedicate themselves can (and do) end up destroying their own immune systems and so becoming more susceptible to disease, or even bringing on autoimmune diseases. People who approach relationships with a need to control or a fear of intimacy end up sabotaging those relationships and their own happiness. People who are stressed and afraid *in general* pull down their own health and ability to enjoy life.

Fear is a mean, ugly liar. It will stab you in the back every time.

In our own day, one disturbing way in which fear steals life is in the substitution of virtual reality for reality. God has given us all needs, desires, and dreams that are meant to propel us out of our comfort zones and into taking action—they are meant to give us a reason to overcome fear. But today's virtual world gives us a way to *feel* like we are meeting those needs and fulfilling those drives when we're not. We might substitute Facebook for community; video games for accomplishment; watching the news for study and learning; pornography for intimacy. These things require zero risk from us (or so we think), but they will hit the same pleasure centers in our brain that actually forming relationships, daring risks, or learning new skills would hit.

We're trading gold for tinsel. When we live in this way we are literally wasting our lives.

Fear is not harmless. It takes form, and those forms can be deadly.

The Thief and the Good Shepherd

Fear shuts down and cripples our lives. It steals life from us. By contrast, God desires to empower us, open our lives up to higher and better things, and give us life.

Jesus compared us to sheep who live in a good shepherd's fold:

> I assure you: I am the door of the sheep. If anyone enters by Me, he will be saved [i.e. rescued, made safe] and will come in and go out and find pasture. A thief comes only to steal and to kill and to destroy. I have come so that they may have life and have it in abundance. I am the good shepherd. (John 10:7, 9-11)

The picture here is a life of access, resources, and freedom that is also bounded by safety and protection. Jesus's wording draws in part on Psalm 23, the most famous song of the shepherd-king David:

> The LORD is my shepherd;
> I shall not want.
> He makes me to lie down in green pastures;
> He leads me beside the still waters.
> He restores my soul;
> He leads me in the paths of righteousness
> For His name's sake.
> *Yea, though I walk through the valley of the shadow of death,*
> *I will fear no evil;*

For You are with me;

Your rod and Your staff, they comfort me. (NKJV)

Notice the familiar language here: evil does not need to be feared, not because it isn't there, but because the Lord is with his people. Like in Jesus's parable, David presents life in God's sheepfold as one of abundance: under the care of the Good Shepherd, there is plenty of food, water, shelter, rest, and protection.

But Jesus lets us know there is a danger. There is a thief who, if he can, will bring panic in order to scatter the sheep and make them vulnerable. The goal is to give him access to the flock so he can steal, kill, and destroy. Of all the threats to abundant life, fear is perhaps the most powerful.

Fear Is a Real Thing

Although fear may begin as a kind of emotional or even physical instinct, it takes shape

> OF ALL THE THREATS TO ABUNDANT LIFE, FEAR IS PERHAPS THE MOST POWERFUL.

and becomes a controlling force in our thoughts. It's on the level of our thoughts that we most need to deal with fear—and that's where we're most equipped to do so.

Rachel's Story: In 2014 I dropped dead of a sudden cardiac arrest. It's a long story . . . suffice it to say, God provided rescue and here I am.

The arrest was traumatic for people around me, but for me, it actually wasn't. I can't remember much about that day, and I woke up in the hospital two days later with a ton of grace and peace. I've never really experienced fear in connection with the whole event.

But because of it, I had a device installed: it's a pacemaker with an internal defibrillator, which means if my heart stops again, it will shock me back to life. You know, like in the movies when they get those big electric pads and they all yell "clear" and the person's body comes right off the table from the jolt. One of those, but on the inside of me.

Last summer I went for a jog. As I was running I was actually quoting Scripture to myself: "Yea, though I walk through the valley of the shadow of death, I will fear no evil, for thou art with me."

And something happened that caused the defib to misfire. Somehow it read my high heart rate as a "bad rhythm" and tried to treat it when it shouldn't have. The voltage knocked me completely off my feet, and it went off nine times in succession while I was trying to get back to the house. I didn't know why it was going off or when (or if) it would stop. It was painful and traumatizing, and it led to another weekend in the hospital.

This has brought a lot of fear. It's gotten into my dreams. It affects me every time I exercise and every time I want to do something fun that could get my heart rate up. To be clear, the doctors tell me I can do anything I want to do, and that my heart handles stress just fine. But still . . . I don't feel like that's true. I fight a constant battle, where fear tells me something terrible could happen, and I tell fear that I trust in God and that I won't allow it to control my life.

The reality is, something bad could happen. I got defibrillated due to a malfunction. It shouldn't have happened, so even though they reset the machine and it shouldn't misfire again, there's no guarantee of that. But the Lord is my shepherd, and I don't have to fear—because he is with me.

If I allow fear to control my life, I'll stop exercising. I'll damage my health for sure that way. I'll stop hiking, I'll stop riding roller coasters, I'll stop doing things that bring me life and joy. I'll impoverish and limit my own experience of life.

But I don't have to let fear dictate my limits. Last September I got on a zip line in the mountains on the state line of California and Nevada, and I zipped nearly a mile down the mountainside at 50 MPH. Not because I'm crazy. Because the truth is I have nothing to fear.

Christian neuroscientist Dr. Caroline Leaf writes in her book *Switch on Your Brain,* "Thoughts are real, physical things that occupy mental real estate. Moment by moment, every day, you are changing the structure of your brain through your thinking."

She explains:

As you think, you choose, and as you choose, you cause genetic expression to happen in your brain. This means you make proteins, and these proteins form your thoughts . . . Eric R. Kandel, a Nobel Prize-winning neuropyschiatrist for his work on memory, shows how our thoughts, even our imaginations, get "under the skin" of our DNA and can turn certain genes on and certain genes off, changing the structure of the neurons in the brain. So as we think and imagine, we change the structure of our brains . . . our thoughts have remarkable power to change the brain. Our brain is changing moment by moment as we are thinking. By our thinking and choosing, we are rede-fining the landscape of our brain. (Dr. Caroline Leaf, *Switch On Your Brain*)

Thoughts are not "nothing"; they have physical substance and physical consequences. Not only do they (literally!) rewire our brains, they also direct our actions, influence our emotions, and shape who we become. Prov-erbs 23:7 was startlingly accurate when it stated several thousand years ago that as an individual thinks, so he is.

Dr. Leaf's research has led her to conclude that "we are wired for love with a natural optimism bias." Thoughts of trust, hope, optimism, and love are healthy. They map our brains in healthy ways and make our bodies healthy as well. Thoughts of fear, bitterness, unforgiveness, and other negatives are, in her words, "toxic thoughts." They literally create unhealthy brains and bodies.

But we have free will. We choose.

We will all feel fear at times. The question is, how we will we respond, particularly in our thought lives? Again, feelings are not the key here. It's not a question of whether you feel fear or not. Jesus in the garden of Gethsemane, sweating blood and weeping for hours in the night, almost certainly felt fear. In fact, that's the dominant emotion seen in the story. But he did not choose to act in fear: he chose surrender to the Father's will and trust in him. He aligned his mind ("Not my will but yours") and did it afraid.

In the book of Revelation, "cowards" are among those pictured on the wrong side of the final judgment, along with murderers, adulterers, idolators, and others. That doesn't sit comfortably with most of us, because we really want to be able to claim fear as a valid excuse. We can't help it if we're scared; that's just human. But the implication of cowards coming under judgment is that a choice has been made that was sin—that was wrong. Fear and unbelief are actually correlated: if we allow fear to control our lives, it is a choice not to trust God.

Jesus urges us to enter "through the door," to live our lives in him so that we can come in, go out, and find pasture—so that we can live abundant lives and cheat the thief. Paul takes a more militant stance: it is our job as believers, he tells us in 2 Corinthians 10:5, to "take every thought captive to the obedience of Christ." Earlier in the same verse he describes this in more detail: "We demolish arguments and every high-minded thing that is raised up against the knowledge of God." This surely applies to more than just fear, but in the war for the mind, fear is a primary opponent.

Just as fear is not neutral, the battle to take back the ground of the mind is not passive. It's an active choice and one that needs to be made over and over again and continually carried out.

> JUST AS FEAR IS NOT NEUTRAL, THE BATTLE TO TAKE BACK THE GROUND OF THE MIND IS NOT PASSIVE.
>
> IT'S AN ACTIVE CHOICE.

The battle isn't easy and victory isn't usually immediate. Especially if we have given a lot of ground to fear in the past, taking back the land is a process. It's important to state here that you won't win all the time . . . and that's okay. Proverbs 24:16 tells us, "Though a righteous man falls seven times, he will get up, but the wicked will stumble into ruin."

If you struggle with paralyzing fear, it's the "try" that matters. Don't allow condemnation to paralyze you too. What matters is that you keep walking with God, trying again, and renewing your faith that God is with you. Ultimately, he will win the victory.

"When my heart is overwhelmed," David wrote—

making it transparently obvious that he did feel overwhelmed and defeated on many occasions—"lead me to the rock that is higher than I" (Psalm 61:2, KJV).

Galatians 6:7-9 says:

Don't be deceived: God is not mocked. For whatever a man sows he will also reap, because the one who sows to his flesh will reap corruption from the flesh, but the one who sows to the Spirit will reap eternal life [i.e. abundant life, the eternal quality of life] from the Spirit. So we must not get tired of doing good, for we will reap at the proper time if we don't give up.

This is a powerful promise: if you continually "sow to the Spirit" and don't give up, planting truth, trust, and hope in your mind and pulling up the weeds of fear from the past, God will absolutely make sure you reap abundant, eternal life. He is staking his own reputation on it.

Taking Back Our Inner Territory

When Jesus began his ministry, his central message was "Repent, for the kingdom of God is here." In Matthew 5:3, he declared that this is a kingdom given even to those who are utterly impoverished within:

> The poor in spirit are blessed, for the kingdom of heaven is theirs.

Being given a kingdom means being given dominion or authority from God. Our dominion is first over our inner lives and then over the way our inner lives manifest in the world. This is why "self-control" is listed as a fruit of the Spirit in Galatians 5 and why we are charged with the responsibility (and power) to take our thoughts captive and renew our minds (see Romans 12:2). It's also why the first step to entry is repentance, which means we take responsibility for ourselves (you can't play the victim and repent) and choose to go in a new direction.

Most of us have a lot of inner territory that needs retaking for the kingdom. Going back to the garden analogy of Galatians 6, we've done a lot of sowing to the flesh in the past, and as a result there's a lot of stuff growing in our lives that needs to be pulled up and replaced. (You may find there's stuff growing you didn't even plant—what we might call "generational sins" or the traumas caused by others.) But we possess all we need to do a good job of this. We have the blood of Christ to cleanse us from the past. We have the Holy Spirit within us to empower and guide us. We have kingdom seeds, in the form of the truth of the Word of God, that we can plant. We also have the promise of blessing, which means God himself will water and empower those seeds to grow.

Releasing Our Excuses

When it comes to taking dominion, it's important for us to accept that the only thing we can control is our own reactions and decisions. We are the limit of our own dominion.

As human beings, we use a lot of excuses that relate to what other people will or won't do, or what circumstances are or are not in our favor. But we do not have dominion over any of this. We can't control other people, and we can't control what happens to us. We're not supposed to. We have dominion over ourselves, period. We often cop out by blaming others, but we are all on equal footing in this regard!

In his audio course "How to Be an Entrepreneur," businessman Eben Pagan teaches that it's essential to train ourselves to say "I am responsible," no matter what happens. This is not the same thing as saying "this is my fault." That is a dead-end statement just as much as excuses are dead-end statements (and it's often inaccurate anyway—lots of things happen to us that are not our fault). But if you will say "I am responsible," then your mind will go to work on what you can do to move forward from any given place, rather than going into an endless loop of blame and excuses that will leave you stuck.

The fact is, victim mentalities don't work. They keep us stuck and stopped. They are the opposite of taking dominion: rather than saying "I am responsible," sowing to the Spirit, and reaching out to the God-who-is-with-us, a victim mentality gives up dominion to others, to the past, and to circumstances. It's a completely dead-end street.

The alternative is dominion: accepting responsibility for yourself, accessing the power that doesn't come from you but has been delegated to you by God, and making new choices that give you life.

Take back the ground of your inner life. Receive dominion and authority from God and stake your claim: from now on, this ground belongs to Yahweh. Everything that comes in or out has to go through the door, which is Jesus. The giants must fall, high things must be torn down, and weeds must be pulled up.

Finally, get busy planting the ground with new seeds: seeds that will give you a kingdom harvest.

Fear is real estate, but so is trust. It's time to replace the old gods of anxiety, worry, and fear with a new master—a Good Shepherd who is here with life abundant.

4
Chapter

CONTROL IS AN ILLUSION

When we get serious about taking dominion, we're likely to run into a counterfeit, one that fully intends to kick the door to fear right back open if we listen to it. That counterfeit is control.

Dominion is not control. Having authority does not mean being in control. Control is not a good or a natural state for any human being ever, except in the very limited sense of having self-control (which is perhaps better described as "being self-disciplined"—as Jesus so aptly pointed out in Matthew 6:27, "Can any of you by worrying make yourself grow by even one inch?" We're not "in control" of ourselves, let alone anything or anyone else).

At its ugliest, control is blatantly destructive. It destroys relationships, it destroys churches, it destroys business. Anything overcontrolled or micromanaged will shrivel up and die. Control can lead to self-destructive behaviors like cutting, where we try to assert some kind of control when we feel like we have none. And the need to control *will keep us in fear,* because we will be afraid when we feel out of control.

The truth is, control is always an illusion. We never have control, though we do sometimes have the perception of it. *Our fearlessness must be based not on our own power in a situation but on God's.*

The Rock Who Ran

Throughout the gospels, Peter stands out among the disciples. He's always the first one to talk, the first one to act, the first one to declare undying faith and loyalty. Even in the sparse writing style of the gospels, his personality is larger than life. He is bold, confident, and apparently fearless. At his worst he's blustery. At his best he's the man Jesus called "the rock."

So it's shocking when, in the moment of crisis, Peter falls apart. His denial of Jesus is one of the most painful moments in the New Testament. This is a man who vehemently declared that he would die with Jesus, and now he's acting like a total coward, lying and swearing when his accuser is no one more intimidating than a teenage girl.

That part of the story is familiar. But the more important part might be what happened just a little earlier, in the garden of Gethsemane. According to the gospel accounts, Judas Iscariot showed up with a cohort to arrest Jesus—a full cohort was roughly six hundred men. Likely Judas didn't bring an entire cohort, but the group was sizeable—probably several hundred. They came at night, in a situation where the disciples were all physically drained and emotionally exhausted. Jesus himself had been up for hours, sweating blood and weeping.

It wasn't exactly anyone's finest hour.

And yet, Peter didn't flinch. In front of *several hundred armed men,* he grabbed a sword and sprang to Jesus's defense. He started a fight. He did it fully aware that his own faithful companions numbered exactly eleven, and that was including Jesus.

What this tells us is that Peter wasn't lying when he said he was willing to die with Jesus. He was. He tried to do it.

But then Jesus told him to put his sword away. Jesus

healed the one man Peter had managed to strike. Jesus ended the battle and went willingly into custody.

Which means he took all the control out of Peter's hands.

That's when Peter lost it.

On some level, Peter's faith wasn't in God after all. It was in his own boldness, his own strength, his own sword, and most of all, *his own understanding of God's plan.* He likely expected God to send angels to help him in that battle. After all, he believed God was about to set up his kingdom physically on earth, with Peter as the rock—the foundation—on which he would build his church.

To end up disarmed, confused, and embarrassed right at the moment of his greatest courage and self-sacrifice was more than Peter could take.

Frankly, I'm not sure any of us would have done any better.

How to Walk on Water

As long as we harbor a need to be in control, trusting in ourselves rather than in God, we are vulnerable to the dominance of fear.

An earlier episode from Peter's life is a vivid example of this. The disciples were out on a boat in the late hours of the night, crossing the rough Sea of Galilee, when they saw someone walking on the water. They thought it was a ghost at first, and were naturally afraid. But Jesus called out to them not to fear.

What happened next is one of the Bible's most memorable stories:

"Lord, if it's You," Peter answered Him, "command me to come to You on the water."

"Come!" He said.

And climbing out of the boat, Peter started walking on the water and came toward Jesus. But when he saw the strength of the wind, he was afraid. And beginning to sink he cried out, "Lord, save me!"

Immediately Jesus reached out His hand, caught hold of him, and said to him, "You of little faith, why did you doubt?" When they got into the boat, the wind ceased. Then those in the boat worshiped Him and said, "Truly You are the Son of God!" (Matthew 14:28-33)

With his eyes on Jesus, Peter did the impossible—

he walked on water. But for a moment, his attention shifted, and he "saw the strength of the wind." It wasn't like Peter didn't know beforehand that there was a wind. According to Matthew, the disciples had been out on the water wrestling this exact same wind for hours; they couldn't get to shore because it was "battering" their boat. But he took his eyes off Jesus, put them on the wind and waves, and realized just how much he wasn't in control of this situation. He wasn't in control of the wind, wasn't in control of the water, wasn't in control of his own ability to walk on a substance people can't walk on.

The result is pretty plain: "He was afraid." And so he began to sink.

Of course, Jesus caught him right away. And the fact that Peter sank doesn't negate the fact that he also walked on water. His boldness and courage got him out of the boat; his relationship with Jesus pulled him out the waves. The episode of fear in the middle did cause him to sink, but ultimately the whole event must have built his faith, not destroyed it.

Life is like this: a lot of false starts, failed tries, and near misses. Yet it's only when we're willing to risk all of that that we can really get out of the boat, develop a history with God, and begin to grow our faith from "little" to "great." That's how you walk on water.

Most of us would rather it didn't work that way. There's a reason the biblical virtue of patience (also called "endurance") isn't popular. Among authors there's a saying: Most people don't want to write, they just want to have written. People naturally want to skip process— we just want to get the result. But like in the case of lottery winners who can't hang onto their money because they've never learned, through the process of making money, how to manage it, it's the process that actually enables and produces the result. You literally can't have the result without the process. You will never learn to walk on water if you don't sink a few times and experience God catching you. The servant who received only one talent buried his money because he was afraid of process and the risks it entails. If he had embraced the process instead, it would have involved a learning curve and probably some losses—but in the end it would have led to multiplication.

We can't embrace process without surrendering control, because we are never, ever in control of our own growth. We can make good decisions and plant good seeds, but we'll always have to trust God with the outcome.

The Power of Surrender

Life can be scary. It is big, it is full of unknowns, and it does bring legitimate pain and confusion at times. Early on, many of us learn that the way to circumvent the scariness and not be afraid is to be in control. But as we've already seen, that's an illusion.

So if we can't be in control, where do we find the courage to step forward in life? How do we stop fear from overwhelming us?

> WE NEED TO TAKE JESUS'S HAND. BUT OFTEN, THIS MEANS WE NEED TO SIMULTANEOUSLY LET GO OF CONTROL.

The answer is that we find it in the One who is in control, in God, who is with us.

We don't get free from fear by controlling circumstances, other people, or even ourselves, but by trusting God to be God in our lives and to be with us always, no matter what. We need to take Jesus's hand. But often, this means we need to simultaneously let go of control. We can't both be God. Either God is God in our lives, or we are.

Jesus's own experience in Gethsemane illustrates

this. On the same night that Peter temporarily lost his faith, Jesus experienced his greatest triumph of faith—when he stared the worst, most visceral fear down and overcame it through trust and surrender.

Jesus knew he was going to die, and he knew it was going to be brutal. He knew there would be spiritual dynamics at play that could be more horrendous than even the physical pain as he took the sins of the world on his body and "became a curse for us" (Galatians 3:13). He knew he would face mockery and accusation and the worst of human nature. It's easy to say "Yeah, well, he was God, it wasn't that hard for him"; but Scripture tells us he experienced the emotions any other human being would:

> Then they came to a place named Gethsemane, and He told His disciples, "Sit here while I pray." He took Peter, James, and John with Him, *and He began to be deeply distressed and horrified.* Then He said to them, *"My soul is swallowed up in sorrow—to the point of death.* Remain here and stay awake." Then He went a little farther, fell to the ground, and began to pray that if it were possible, the hour might pass from Him. And He said, "Abba, Father! All things are possible for You. Take this cup away from Me. Nevertheless, not what I will, but what You will." (Mark 14:32-36)

Mark tells us that Jesus repeated the same prayer three times. Each time he asked the Father to change the plans. We're told that he was so physically distressed that he sweat blood. The horror Jesus experienced as he faced into the future was profound.

Yet, it was his decision every time to relinquish control and surrender to the Father's will that made it possible for him to endure the cross. Jesus did in fact go through a horrible, brutal death. He experienced the effects of sin and separation from the Father. He went through excruciating pain mentally, physically, and emotionally.

But he did it without wavering, because he didn't claim control in the situation. He simply surrendered. It was the one thing Peter didn't do.

Take Up Your Cross and Follow Me

When Jesus was coaching his disciples in how to follow God, he put out a provocative call:

Then Jesus said to His disciples, "If anyone wants to come with Me, he must deny himself, take up his cross, and follow Me. For whoever wants to save his life will lose it, but whoever loses his life because of Me will find it." (Matthew 16:24-25)

What does this mean? After all, we don't have literal physical crosses to pick up, and the rest of Scripture doesn't really allow us to make this call about arbitrarily punishing ourselves in some way. Rather, this verse is about making a decision ahead of time that you will go all the way. It's a preemptive surrender: I will completely relinquish control and follow Jesus even if it kills me.

The power of preemptive surrender is hard to measure. Andy Falleur, pastor of Calvary Chapel Ottawa, once compared "taking up one's cross" to a fireman who joins the force or a soldier who joins the army. They decide, at the moment they sign up, that if it comes to down to it, they will die. They don't have to make a decision in the moment as to whether they will go into a burning building or march into battle. They make the decision to lay down their lives the same day they sign up.

That is the most effective way to lead the Christian life as well. Decide, from day one, to surrender it all. Make life about obedience, not control.

Doing this has many effects, but one of them is that it pulls the stinger out of fear. When you've already given up everything, what do you have left to lose?

Fourfold Faith

The Greek word translated "faith," *pistis,* has four different facets. Put all together, they give a clear picture of what faith really is. *Pistis* means faith in the sense of a set of beliefs or truths; what we might call "the Christian faith." It also means belief—"what you say, I believe." It also means trust, in the sense of personally trusting someone. And finally, it also means faithfulness, or full commitment.

We earlier connected fear of the Lord to loyalty, and here again we see that connection. To fear the Lord is to be loyal to him, and to be loyal to him is to believe and trust him.

Talk of surrender and obedience can be disheartening because we may feel like we aren't capable of fully surrendering or obeying. But that takes us back to process and the need to be willing to risk. It's important to know that God is okay with risk: the master in the parable of the talents praised the two servants who risked, even though they risked *more* than the one-talent servant even had in the first place, because they did it out of an understanding of who the master was and what he wanted.

Jesus caught Peter when he started to sink, and over

the years he reprimanded him many times—he even called him "Satan" once. But he also named him "the rock," promised to build his church on Peter's foundation, and ultimately entrusted him with leadership of the early church and the beginning of the missions movement to the rest of the world.

Peter's messy middle didn't disqualify him. The only thing that could have disqualified him would have been if he had never tried.

Jesus was once asked how people could do the works of God. He said, "This is the work of God—that you believe [*pistis*—believe/trust/commit] in the One He has sent" (John 6:29). For Jesus, believing is obeying. Trust is obeying. Loyalty is obeying.

There's a tendency in our world to equate obedience with a kind of mindless "jumping to," just following orders. But that's not how the Bible talks about it. In Scripture, obedience is heavily relational. It's about allegiance and learning to share God's mind. Even the word for *obedience* comes from a root that indicates "to hear." Only someone who is in relationship with God and is listening to him can obey.

Dr. Michael S. Heiser, in his book *Unseen Realms,* sums up the biblical picture even in the Old Testament:

The core of the law was fidelity to Yahweh alone, above all gods. To worship other gods was to demonstrate the absence of belief, love, and loyalty. Doing the works of the law without having the heart aligned only to Yahweh was inadequate. This is why the promise of the possession of the promised land is repeatedly and inextricably linked in the Torah to the first two commandments (i.e. staying clear of idolatry and apostasy).

The history of Israel's kings illustrates the point. King David was guilty of the worst of crimes against humanity in the incident with Bathsheba and Uriah the Hittite (2 Sam 11). He was clearly in violation of the law and deserving of death. Nevertheless, his belief in who Yahweh was among all gods never wavered. God was merciful to him, sparing him from death, though his sin had consequences the rest of his life. But there was no doubt that David was ever a believer in Yahweh and never worshiped another. Yet other kings of Israel and Judah were tossed aside and both kingdoms sent into exile—because they worshiped other gods. Personal failure, even of the worst kind, did not send the nation into exile. Choosing other gods did.

The same is true in the New Testament. Believing

the gospel means believing that Yahweh, the God of Israel, came to earth incarnated as a man, voluntarily died on the cross as a sacrifice for our sin, and rose again on the third day. That is the content of our faith this side of the cross. Our believing loyalty is demonstrated by our obedience to "the law of Christ" (1 Cor 9:21; Gal 6:2). We cannot worship another. Salvation means believing loyalty to Christ, who was and is the visible Yahweh. There is no salvation in any other name (Acts 4:12), and faith must remain intact (Rom 11:17-24; Heb 3:19; 10:22, 38-39). Personal failure is not the same as trading Jesus for another god—and God knows that. (Michael S. Heiser, *Unseen Realm*)

The obedience God is after is not a set of works or a flawless performance, it's a deep relational loyalty. This is how we can best understand the role of free will in our lives. Free will is a good gift from God, not a trick. God is not a puppet master and doesn't want our puppet strings. Rather, he wants mature children who make decisions out of love and loyalty to him—and he is endlessly patient with our process of maturation.

Philosopher and theologian Keith Ward says, "Free will is a place where people can decide to do what is right or to do what is wrong, and nothing determines their choice—lots of things influence their choice, but nothing determines it except them." Exercising our free will within our personal realm of dominion within the kingdom of God is the ultimate expression of faith, love, and loyalty.

Control vs Dominion

When we trust in Christ, we are given a kingdom. This means that God delegates authority to us, the ability to take dominion.

> SURRENDER TO GOD, DOESN'T MEAN BEING PASSIVE OR FATALISTIC ABOUT OUR LIVES.

We've already seen that this doesn't mean controlling anything. We can't control others, circumstances, or really anything . . . nor are we supposed to. Instead, our default attitude is to be one of surrender to God.

Surrender to God, however, *doesn't* mean being passive or fatalistic about our lives. We have dominion and are expected to use it!

So what is dominion?

- Dominion is the ability to make right choices —to choose life.

• Dominion is authority over our own mindset (our inner life). We are told to "Love the Lord your God with all your heart, mind, soul, and strength" (Mark 12:30). We are told to "take every thought captive" (2 Corinthians 10:5). These are very proactive things only we can do. No one else can do this for us. It's in our realm of authority.

• We are given dominion over the earth. This is sometimes called the "creation mandate." The creation mandate was given to human beings in Genesis 2, immediately after they were created. They were "to be fruitful and multiply, fill the earth and subdue it." This is classically understood in terms of culture creation, and it ties in closely with the parable of the talents. The idea is that we have the responsibility and the power to make a positive impact in the world through creative and governing means.

Dominion means you have the right and ability of response; you are "response-able." Again, you don't have *control.* You can plant seeds, in your life and in the world around you, but you can't force a crop to come up. It's your job to cultivate the soil of your heart and plant the seeds. This is our responsibility. And yet in our own strength, there is absolutely nothing we can do to cause the seeds to grow. God is the only one who can do that.

Circle of Influence vs Circle of Concern

When we don't understand our own domain, we can become crippled by the pressure of things that are outside of it. This is especially true in our information-glutted age, when everyone is hyperconnected and we can watch real-time video of someone on the other side of the planet suffering or starving or cutting someone else's head off. The needs and threats are overwhelming.

On top of this, much of the media deliberately feeds fear. It's how they keep ratings high and people tuning in. That's why these days it seems like every winter flurry turns into "Snowmageddon," and economic collapse is always imminent, and terrorists are overrunning the nation (even though you are still more likely, in North America, to die from slipping in the bathtub than you are in a terrorist attack), and you should be afraid of your neighbor, the flu, and your facial cream, pretty much in equal measure. So much of what we allow to be poured into our thought lives is deliberately designed to make us afraid.

There are several problems going on here, but we want to highlight two.

First, fear lies. It just flat-out doesn't agree with reality much of the time. Most of what you fear will never happen.

As an example, one of the most paralyzing fears in our modern society is the fear of scarcity. We constantly feel like there isn't enough—not enough for us, not enough to go around, not enough to sustain us much longer, just not enough. We're going to run out: out of oil, out of energy, out of money, out of family, just out.

Yet the fact is, we live in the midst of the greatest abundance available to any generation of human beings ever. Even the poorest people in our society have access to more resources than most people throughout history have had.

Second, much of what the media presents to us to fear and worry about is outside of our domain—the area where we have dominion.

Stephen Covey teaches on this using what he calls the "Circle of Concern" vs the "Circle of Influence." Our circle of concern is potentially enormous. It includes anything that, if we hear about it, will concern us. Examples of things in our circle of concern might be the proliferation of cancers in the modern world, or what somebody in Pakistan believes, or economic collapse in Greece.

(There are some people for whom this stuff isn't circle-of-concern information; it's circle of influence. But we'll get there in a minute.)

The media is an open floodgate for circle-of-concern kinds of information. So is social media. So might be your local hair salon, or anywhere you happen to hear a lot of gossip and conjecture.

Your circle of concern is anything that might worry you *that you can't do anything about.*

Your circle of influence, on the other hand, is much smaller. It includes anything that might concern you *that you can do something about.*

The state of marriages in North America is your circle of concern. The state of *your* marriage is your circle of influence; you can't control it, but you can do something about it. Unless you are a doctor or medical researcher, worldwide cancer is your circle of concern. Your own health is your circle of influence. You can't do anything about economic collapse in Greece (unless your circle of influence happens to include the Greek economy) but you can make wise financial decisions in your own life.

In biblical terms, what's inside your circle of influence is the stuff in your domain. This is where your ability to make choices and act on them, to respond, to plant seed, to choose life, is significant and effective.

Here's why this is important: if we don't distinguish between the circles, we will end up ineffective because the circle of concern, huge and overwhelming as it is, will drain our energy and our focus. It will leave us emotionally exhausted and *fearful*.

One of us had a conversation recently with someone who refused to do anything because of things she had heard on the news. There were things she wanted to do with her life (things inside her circle of influence), but she felt paralyzed by circle-of-concern stuff. She built walls around her life, boxing herself in with "I could never" and "People are dangerous" and "Traffic accidents are at an all-time high" and "You can catch swine flu if you travel." We may not all be so extreme, but in the modern world, we are all affected by too much information to some degree or other. We have to decide where to draw the lines in our own lives—what we will allow to limit us, stop us, worry us, or affect us.

Our point isn't that information is bad or that we shouldn't care about what happens in other parts of the world. Our point is that we need to let God be God, and we need to be diligent to take authority in the areas where we actually have dominion. If we all did this, the world's problems would be solved. If we all addressed our area of dominion with kingdom principles and the truths of God, the kingdom would come on earth—which is precisely what Jesus came to make happen.

It's an observable phenomenon that when we do exercise authority and influence, our circle of influence grows. This is evident in the parable of the talents: those who invested their talents well and made back double were given more. And because they had embraced process and risk, they were able to manage the more.

When we allow ourselves to be overwhelmed by things outside our dominion and never take dominion where we can and should, we end up trapped inside walls of our own creation. We can't grow, we can't move, we can't enjoy life, we can't make a difference or take opportunities.

Into our world's troubled realities, Jesus says, "In this world you will have trouble, but take heart, for I have overcome the world" (John 16:33, NIV). The King James Version has him saying "Be of good cheer."

Jesus can be so outrageously cheerful about a world full of troubles because he wasn't looking at the strength of the wind; he was looking at the Father. The Bible never discounts the reality of trouble and evil in the world;

the reason not to be afraid is the presence of God.

You can get yourself psyched up that nothing bad will happen, but the problem with that is that as soon as something bad does happen, your mental victory will come crashing down. Our faith needs to be in God, not in any set of circumstances; and specifically that God will be with us, not that he will prevent anything bad from ever happening.

The End of the Story

For Peter, the ups and downs of a faith journey resulted in a man who could stand under immense pressure. In Acts 4, the same Peter who lost his courage in the face of a servant girl stood up in front of the most powerful and respected men in his nation, after he'd been hauled in and jailed for street preaching and healing in Jesus's name, and asked them, "You judge for yourselves whether it's right for us to obey men rather than God. We can do what you want, but we're going to keep preaching." He did. Later he bucked thousands of years of tradition, pressure from his fellow church leaders, and his own understanding to become the first evangelist to the Gentile world. He led the church through severe persecution and intense internal conflict.

Even later, he finally took up his cross and followed Jesus, crucified by the Romans.

But before all that, two things happened. The first was that Jesus was resurrected. The second was that just as he did when Peter started to sink on the water, Jesus reached out his hand and pulled Peter back up.

In a private conversation on a beach, recorded in John 21, Jesus asked him three times, "Peter, do you love me?"

When Peter said yes, Jesus nodded and entrusted Peter with his greatest treasure: "Feed my lambs."

Peter betrayed Jesus because he couldn't handle the fear of being out of control. Later, he faithfully followed Jesus—because love, obedience, and process had overcome fear.

5
Chapter

LEARNING TO STAND ALONE

In an earlier chapter we read the story of Joshua, one of the Bible's most fearless individuals. Joshua and his friend Caleb were two of twelve spies sent into the land of Canaan to scout it out. When they came back, though, they were horrified to hear the other ten spies tell the people of the nation that they could not possibly enter the land, because its inhabitants were "stronger than we are."

Referencing the giants they had seen there, the spies told the people, "To ourselves we seemed like grasshoppers, and we must have seemed the same to them" (Numbers 13:31, 33).

This was not at all the perspective of Joshua and Caleb. They had scouted out the land with gratitude and excitement. The land was everything God had said it would be and more. This was the promise to their ancestors fulfilled. They were more than ready to go in! The last thing they felt like was "grasshoppers."

We've already seen that Joshua and Caleb were in the minority—so much so that they alone of their generation were allowed to enter the land. They were in fact part of a tiny handful of people in Israel who truly feared the Lord, a tiny community within the larger community of Israel that included Moses.

Growing Up in Faith

When Moses first appeared to the nation of Israel back in Egypt and declared that Yahweh had sent him to deliver them, he wasn't received warmly. Most of the Israelites doubted him, and with reason. But Moses performed miracles in the name of the Lord and gave the people many reasons to adopt his faith. Yahweh truly had come down to set them free. All the Israelites really had to do was wait out the turmoil of the transition while Moses did the heavy lifting. It was Moses and Aaron confronting Pharaoh, turning the Nile to blood, and issuing Yahweh's commands.

In the beginning of our faith journey, especially if we are born into Christian homes, many of us borrow others' faith and rely on them to counteract our fear. We do this as children: we don't need to rely on God for ourselves much; we can just rely on our parents, who rely on God. We do it as young people in the church: we can rely on pastors or youth leaders to hear from God for us; we don't so much need to do it on our own. As long as they are confident, so are we. Like Joshua and Caleb in Egypt, watching Moses take a stand and be bold and courageous, we just watch, wait, and follow the leader.

This is natural, and it's not necessarily bad. It's like using training wheels when you're learning to ride a bike. But part of the process of growing up is learning to locate our courage not in others but in our own connection with God. At some point we have to move from relying on others to being able to stand alone.

This is what we see in the moment of the spies' report. Joshua and Caleb seem caught off guard by the faithless, fearful responses of their fellow spies. But the nation as a whole is quick to agree with the other ten.

Think for a moment of the peer pressure inherent in this situation. Here are people you usually expect to stand with you, instead making a decision you disagree with—and there are tens of thousands of them. There was tremendous pressure from this "community of faith" to call Moses a liar and head back to Egypt. And after all, there were giants in the land. Everyone else saw the giants as a huge (pardon the pun) problem.

It would be enough to make anyone question their own judgment. It's hard to be brave. It's even harder when everybody around you is afraid.

But Joshua and Caleb took a stand. They stood alone, in a very public, very vulnerable way. If you recall, they were nearly stoned along with Moses.

Earlier, we made the case that Joshua (and Caleb as well) was able to almost completely transcend normal fear because of how deeply and personally he feared the Lord. His fear of the Lord was love: it was a beautiful meeting of reverence, devotion, and terror. You might say Joshua was in love with Yahweh. After all, isn't that what being in love feels like?

People in love are often willing to do crazy things. Their devotion overrules fear. They will stand alone.

We want to make the case that this is what the Bible means when it talks about holiness.

Perfecting Holiness in the Fear of the Lord

Within the Sinai covenant (what we often call "the law," or the Torah), God gave the nation of Israel a series of restrictions that scholars sometimes call "the Holiness Code." Unlike moral laws such as "Do not kill" and "Do not commit adultery," for the most part, the Holiness Code laws are not really moral directives. The whole purpose of this set of laws was to separate Israel from the nations around them and to cause them to understand, through a series of vivid physical *pictures,* the holiness of God. The rationale for these laws is given in Leviticus 20:26: "Be ye holy, for I am holy" (KJV).

Many of the specific "Holiness Code" laws did not cross over into the New Covenant era. The reason for this is pretty simple: after Jesus came, God began drawing all of the nations into a new covenant with himself and thus did away with the wall of separation between his Jewish children and his Gentile children.

But now in Christ Jesus, you who were far away have been brought near by the blood of the Messiah. For He is our peace, who made both groups one and tore down the dividing wall of hostility. In His flesh, He made of no effect the law consisting of commands and expressed in regulations, so that He might create in Himself one new man from the two, resulting in peace. (Ephesians 2:13-15)

But the requirement that *God's people be holy because he is holy* did not change. In fact, the apostle Peter quotes Leviticus in his first letter to the churches:

As obedient children, do not be conformed to the desires of your former ignorance. But as the One who called you is holy, you also are to be holy in all your conduct; for it is written, Be holy, because I am holy. (1 Peter 1:14-16)

Paul also writes about the need for holiness. In 2 Corinthians 7:1 he writes,

Therefore, having these promises, beloved, let us cleanse ourselves from all filthiness of the flesh and spirit, *perfecting holiness in the fear of God.* (NKJV)

Holiness and the fear of the Lord go hand-in-hand. You might say holiness is the way the fear of the Lord shapes our lives: it is how we will live when we fear the Lord. And so it is holiness that gives us the power to stand alone when others fall away, to walk in loyalty and faith when everyone else around us has become a self-defined grasshopper.

It's holiness that turns ordinary Christians into giant-takers.

What Is Holiness?

We often think of *holiness* as just another word for righteousness, but actually, the words are quite different. Fundamentally, holiness means "otherness." The Hebrew word *kadosh,* "holy," means other, different, transcendent. This is what it means that God is holy. He is entirely other. He is I Am That I Am.

Applied to people or objects, to be holy is to be set apart for something or someone. The Latin word for holy, *sanctus,* gives us the word *sanctification,* which again means to be set apart for a specific purpose or person. (We also get the words *sacred* and *consecrate* from this root.) You might also think of the word *devotion.* Something devoted to a specific purpose is used only for that purpose. Someone devoted to another person lives only for that person. In our case, we are set apart or devoted to God.

To be holy as God is holy is to be set apart, consecrated, and devoted to God and for God. It is to be marked as specially his, and in that way set apart and made different from everyone else in the world.

In the ancient world, most gods were fairly happy to share. Their worshipers didn't need to be devoted to them; they just needed to be faithful to bring sacrifices and offer bribes. Yahweh, by contrast, is a jealous God. He makes this statement multiple times throughout the Bible and compares apostasy to adultery in terms that would make any modern preacher blush.

Deuteronomy 4:24 gives us one of the earliest declarations of God's jealousy: "For the LORD your God is a consuming fire, a jealous God."

If you are holy to the Lord, you are completely set apart for him. Only God gets your worship. On a deep level this means only God gets your fear. Only God gets your loyalty.

> Believing loyalty was therefore not just academic [in the Old Testament]. By definition it must be conscious and active. Israel knew that her God had fought for her and loved her, but the relationship came with expectations. As she embarked for the promised land, Israel would have daily, visible reminders not only of Yahweh's presence but of his total *otherness*. Having the divine presence with you could be both fantastic and frightening. (Michael S. Heiser, *Unseen Realm*)

In the physical pictures of the "holiness code," holiness had three basic practical components:

- It was aligned with life, not death

- It was aligned with wholeness, not brokenness

- It was aligned with purity, not pollution

The language of purification, clean and unclean, was typically used in connection with holiness. For example, among the most famous of the Holiness Code laws are the dietary laws. These are not arbitrary: all of the animals Israel was forbidden to eat on the grounds that they were "unclean" were carnivores, scavengers, or (like pigs) omnivores, which meant they would either kill or else eat dead things. This connection with death made them unclean. A woman's menstrual flow made her unclean, not because she was somehow morally guilty, but because the loss of blood was connected with loss of life. Any Israelite who touched a dead body became unclean.

Those who were ritually unclean had to go through a purification process in order to come into the presence of God in the tabernacle. Those who were permanently unclean or unwhole, because of a defect like a missing limb or a chronic disease like leprosy, could never enter. The message was clear: Yahweh is the perfect, whole, and pure Life-giver. Death and imperfection cannot come into his presence.

This was the key, in fact: holiness was about entering the presence of God and so fellowshipping with him.

In the New Testament, these external requirements are removed. Paul explains that they were always just pictures anyway:

> Therefore let no one judge you in regard to food and drink or in regard to [the observance of] a festival or a new moon or a Sabbath day. Such things are only a shadow of what is to come and they have only symbolic value; but the substance [the reality of what is foreshadowed] belongs to Christ. (Colossians 2:16-17, AMP)

In Jesus, and because we have been purified by his blood sacrifice, we have full access to the presence of God at all times. We are "made perfect," that is, whole and without defect, and "sanctified," that is made holy, set apart for God, by the sacrifice of Jesus for us. See Hebrews 10:1-25 for more about this powerful truth. Verse 14 sums it up well: "For by one offering He has perfected forever those who are sanctified."

How to Be Like God

In Genesis 3, the infamous story of the fall of man, the serpent told Eve that if she ate from the tree of the knowledge of good and evil, her eyes would be opened and she would become "like God." It both was and wasn't a lie—but what's clear is that the enemy never had any intention of mankind's actually becoming more like God. His goal was to make them into animals, slaves to their flesh. He nearly succeeded.

But God has always had a higher vision for the people he created and loves. In Leviticus, he makes it simple: "Be holy, for I am holy." *Be like Me by being set apart for Me.* If we want to be like God, we need to be holy—set apart for him so we can come into his presence, learn from him relationally, and take on his nature more and more.

We are both given holiness as a gift ("perfected forever" and "sanctified") and called to holiness as a way of life (1 Peter 1:16, 2 Corinthians 7:1).

Just before the birth of Jesus, his uncle Zechariah prayed and prophesied over his son John (the Baptist): "That He would grant unto us that we, being delivered out of the hand of our enemies, might serve Him without fear in holiness and righteousness before Him all the days of your life" (NKJV). The Greek word for "holiness" here is *hosiotes,* of which Strong's says, "This is holiness 'fleshed out,' i.e. incarnated by living by faith … as heaven's will works out on earth."

When we live in holiness, heaven meets earth in our lives.

Don't Drink, Don't Chew, and Don't Go with Girls Who Do?

Since holiness is the key to becoming like God (which the enemy never actually wanted for us), it shouldn't be surprising that the concept is under attack in the church and culture today. There was a time when many preachers talked about the need for holiness; nowadays it's not a common message, especially from pulpits that aren't really interested in turning people off.

But why is this? Why is such a powerful and beautiful concept seen as embarrassing or outdated?

The problem isn't with holiness itself. It's with legalism. For many of us, "holiness" has become synonymous with restrictiveness or "old-timeyness." It might call to mind a lot of extrabiblical rules, from "godly women don't wear makeup" to "good Christians don't go to dances" to "only hippies would wear a beard." (Yes, that kind of thinking is still out there—we've personally run into every one of these!) As a result, no trendy, happening church ever wants to bring up the word *holiness* because it has so much baggage.

But this is not the picture given in Scripture. In fact, in the New Testament the holiest people were the ones pushing the boundaries the furthest in terms of allowing Gentiles into the church, removing cultural litmus tests, reading Scripture in brand-new ways, and insisting that God was doing something new. Paul's stance for singleness, for example, was radically nonconservative. So was Peter's willingness to go into a Gentile centurion's house and preach the gospel to him.

Our point here is not that we should push boundaries just to push them, or

> BIBLICAL HOLINESS HAS NO INHERENT CONNECTION TO OLDNESS, OR TRADITION, OR EVEN PARTICULARLY TO RULES. IT'S AN IDENTITY.

that we ought to toss out traditional understandings of Scripture on a whim. It's simply to point out that *biblical holiness* has no inherent connection to oldness, or tradition, or even particularly to rules. It's an identity, a fundamental self-concept, a core understanding of one's self and one's place in the world: *I am not my own; I am set apart for God.*

When we really believe that, and we see ourselves as being specially set apart for God in body, soul, and spirit, we find the courage to live in a way that is profoundly different from those around us.

Holiness Is Not Legalism, and Legalism Is Not Holy

Holiness absolutely includes moral purity. This is because we are set apart for a morally pure God. We are set apart for life, wholeness, and purity.

Where we get confused is when we define holiness in external and particularly cultural terms. This tends to happen in groups, with every group setting its own external (and often arbitrary) standards. One group feels it's holier for their men to shave; another feels it's holier to wear long beards. One group thinks only two-hundred-year-old hymns are holy, while another decides that holiness is a particular type of beat or song arrangement. We start to define holiness by what words you will or won't use, what movies you will or won't watch, what type of clothing you wear or don't wear, whether you drink alcohol or you don't.

The irony is that most of these things become more about fitting in with a particular crowd and having that crowd's approval than they are about being genuinely set apart for God and willing to stand alone. We may be willing to "stand against the culture," but is that because we're holy to the Lord—or because we care most about the approval of our smaller subculture?

When we create legalistic strictures and call them "holiness," we are defining an external litmus test for pleasing God. So if we define holiness as, for example, "modest dress," then as soon as we achieve that according to our culture's standards, we stop. We figure we've hit the mark of holiness—even if we're still jealous, or operating in a controlling spirit, or bitter.

To be clear: a self-concept of being holy will affect what you watch, wear, eat, drink, say, and participate in, because you will understand that none of these things are just about you and your preferences. Everything you do and *are* is about being set apart for God. But it won't be about conforming to a particular cultural pattern.

We end up in legalism when we add to what God says. On the surface this may not seem like a problem. What's wrong with building fences around God's commands? What's wrong with a rule that says Christians should never drink alcohol (even though Jesus did, and so did the apostles)—wouldn't it just keep everyone safe and make sure nobody succumbs to drunkenness or worse, alcoholism?

The problem is that God hasn't said that Christians (as a group) cannot drink. When we add to what God says, we tend to take what he *does say* less seriously and begin majoring on our own interpretations, which leads to disunity and hypocrisy in the church and gives people a reason to discredit our faith. The world can tell when we're just making stuff up.

There's a key here: we often default to legalism because it makes us feel safe. Really understanding and applying God's Word for our own lives and culture feels risky; we might get it wrong. We will definitely be out of control. Our old enemy, fear, is at the root of legalism, which is why legalism tends to go so horribly awry. The legalistic Pharisees, who built fences around every command of God to ensure they couldn't get anywhere close to breaking one, masterminded the crucifixion of God himself.

While the natural outgrowth of holiness is godliness (God-likeness), the natural outgrowth of legalism is pride. The contrast is fascinating: while godliness is connected to humility, honesty, and surrender, pride tells us that we are already like God.

We need to learn to clearly define things as God does. This will allow us to hit the target. If we redefine holiness and righteousness, we redefine the target, so we end up hitting the wrong one.

Holiness Is a Heart Thing

Holiness is a heart matter, not an external appearance. It requires walking some fine lines. We tend to think that if we take things to an extreme we will be closer to what God wants, but anything taken to an extreme becomes a distortion. Holiness is a centering on God, not a pendulum swing in the furthest possible direction.

Paul set "holiness" free from outward pictures and talks instead about postures of the heart. Remember, holiness means being set apart for life, wholeness, and purity. When the Holy Spirit indwells and directs your life, the fruit of holiness is seen in love, joy, peace, patience, kindness, goodness, faith, gentleness, and self-control (Galatians 5:22-23). We are set apart for God in body, soul, and spirit, and so we live in ways that are counterintuitive and not natural to humanity. They flow out of a trusting relationship with God.

This lifestyle of being set apart, valuing what God values and seeking to live in full alignment with his will and character, makes us brave. Fear loses its grip as holiness redefines what is important and what is not.

No Lone Wolves

It's our belief that at some point, every believer will be challenged to stand alone. You will have to have faith when no one else does. You will have to take steps that no one else supports. You will have to step out from the herd.

For whatever reason, human beings have a strong "herd instinct." In a herd, the safest place to be is the middle. When you're right at the point of average and mediocre, you don't stand out, which means you aren't a target. The lions stalking the herd won't single you out.

Even though we're not being stalked by actual predators, for most of us, standing out from the herd is a scary thing. When we get out front or lag behind, we're not protected by the crowd. We're vulnerable: to criticism, to failure, to loss.

For us to walk free of fear and truly embrace holiness, it's absolutely necessary that we learn to step out of the herd. But when we say this, we don't mean that you should disconnect from community. We are not meant to be controlled by a herd mentality—but neither are we meant to be lone wolves.

God has always been about creating community. Immediately after creating Adam, he said, "It isn't good for Adam to be alone; I will make him a helper suited to him." (The word for "helper" is *ezer,* the same word used of the Holy Spirit or of armies every other time it's used in the Old Testament. It's similar to the term used for the Holy Spirit in the New Testament: *paraklete.*) This was within a context where Adam walked with God and probably with angelic beings. He needed someone else— someone human, like him, to be in community with. This wasn't just about marriage; Adam and Eve were to give birth to an entire human community.

Lone-wolf people often say they don't need other people because they have a special relationship with God. On some level they have special revelation, they get visited by angels, they are unique and no one understands them—and all this gives them license to cut themselves off from human relationship and accountability. But God said that *Adam,* who walked with God and had access to the whole heavenly realm, was alone and that it wasn't good. We are meant for *human* community.

Social science declares that you are the average of the five people you hang out with the most. Peer pressure is powerful. The community and family of God is designed to grow us by essentially harnessing peer pressure to pull us up to a higher level. If you were buddies with Caleb and Joshua, you felt pressure to have more faith, to be stronger and more courageous and more loyal to Yahweh.

There's a story in the Old Testament that may illustrate the dangers of a loner mentality. It's about Elijah, one of God's greatest prophets, and it's found in 1 Kings 19. Right after Elijah's astounding victory over the prophets of Baal on Mount Carmel, the queen, Jezebel, threatened his life—and Elijah fled in apparent terror. He holed up in a cave in the wilderness and told God that he wanted to die. It's a bit of a mystery: why was a man who moments ago showed such holy boldness now overcome with fear? He had everything we've been talking about—holiness, fear of the Lord, willingness to step outside his comfort zone.

There may be a clue in what Elijah said to God at this point. *He complained that he was alone.* Jezebel had killed everyone else who was faithful to Yahweh, "and I alone am left." Elijah saw himself as a lone ranger, and something about that drained his courage.

God answered him by telling him that he wrong: "You're not alone. I have preserved seven thousand who have not bowed the knee to Baal."

Embracing Community (While Standing Alone)

In the New Testament, Jesus was surrounded by community from the start. Although Jesus was often called upon to stand alone in obedience to the Father, he was never without community. As a baby he had Mary and Joseph, and Mary's cousin Elizabeth, and their child John, and the support of the prophets Simeon and Anna in the temple. Angels gathered around this family too, often showing up and prophesying, but they also had other human beings who walked with them.

When Jesus began his ministry, he gathered twelve apostles who lived and traveled with him and with each other. They were also accompanied by a group of women, and everywhere they went they created a community of believers. This community then extended into the mission to the Gentiles. Even Paul, whom we might be tempted to see as the New Testament's ultimate lone wolf, constantly gathered people around him. He rarely traveled alone, always traveling with a community and planting communities.

In God, we must learn to become individuals, to stand alone. It's essential that we live holy, set apart uniquely for God, in a way that gives us courage to go against the tide. Yet we must also see ourselves as part of a body, a community. We can't use holiness as a cover for fear of relationship. The body would not function well if the foot tried to be like eyes and see or the kidneys tried to act more like a heart and refused to stand alone in their function, but it would not function at all if all the parts disconnected and tried to act independently of each other.

In Galatians 1:10 Paul asked, "Am I now trying to win the approval of human beings, or of God? Or am I trying to please people? If I were still trying to please people, I would not be a servant of Christ" (NIV). He understood that he was holy—set apart completely for God. There could be no question of giving up ground in order to please people or go with the flow. Yet he dedicated his life to building community: the people of God, spurring one another on to higher and holier things.

You will be called to stand alone at times, even for whole seasons. When you do, it will set you free from fear's control at a whole new level. Standing alone is a reality of life and an essential part of maturing in God. But it's not meant to be an ongoing, continuous lifestyle. It's people who are capable of standing alone who form the healthiest communities—to borrow from nature again, we function best as a pack, not a herd, with everyone playing a role and supporting one another in strength and courage.

6
Chapter

POWER

Since beginning this journey in chapter 1, we've come a long way together. We've talked about some big concepts, like holiness, fear of the Lord, the need to release control, and the serious consequences of giving the throne of our lives over to fear.

But now we want to go back to the beginning. In chapter 1, we shared a key verse with you. It's found in 2 Timothy 1:7: "For God has not given us a spirit of fear, but of power and of love and of a sound mind."

Way back then, we made the case that we aren't asked to overcome fear in our own power. We are given a gift, or more precisely three gifts, through the presence of the Holy Spirit in our lives.

Accessing these gifts will displace fear.

For the next three chapters, we want to unpack these gifts and what they mean in our lives. We'll start with the first: we have been given the spirit of power.

What Is the Spirit of Power?

In the New Testament, two different Greek words are translated "power." The word here in 2 Timothy 1:7 is the less frequent of the two. It's the Greek word *dunamis,* which means strength—the miracle-working *power* of the Holy Spirit. It's the same word behind the English word *dynamite.*

It's not the word for authority or dominion (*exousia*), which is also translated "power"—rather the focus here is on energy or strength. The concepts are related, though: the disciples could work miracles by the *dunamis* of the Holy Spirit because Jesus had given them *exousia* over disease and evil spirits. The disciples were promised "power from on high" when the Holy Spirit came. They would be "clothed with it," baptized—immersed, or as our pastor likes to say, "pickled"—in it.

Dunamis might also be translated "ability." To have the spirit of *dunamis* means "to be able."

As we have already seen, the Greek word for "fear" in 2 Timothy 1:7, *deilia,* stresses the idea of cowardice or timidity. It's our natural, instinctive fear applied too broadly and too indiscriminately, so that we see the potential of harm everywhere, and that fear comes to control us.

Often, we feel afraid because we feel powerless. We feel weak—unable. So fear rises up and convinces us that we can't, we aren't, we lack, we should go back in our little cave and hide.

> OFTEN, WE FEEL AFRAID BECAUSE WE FEEL POWERLESS. SO FEAR RISES UP AND CONVINCES US THAT WE CAN'T.
>
> GOD SAYS THE OPPOSITE.

God says the opposite. He says we are strong; we are able. We have the power of the Holy Spirit, the dynamite strength of Christ. To quote Paul again, "I can do all things through Christ who strengthens me" (Philippians 4:13, NKJV).

Remember Joshua and Caleb at the border of the promised land? They had the spirit of power: "We must go up and take possession of the land because we can certainly conquer it!" (Numbers 13:30).

Why Has God Given Us Power?

The Bible is never dishonest about the very real challenges in the world. It doesn't pretend things are just hunky-dory, easy, and fine. Jesus never said his people wouldn't face trouble. Quite the opposite: "You will have suffering in this world. Be courageous! I have conquered the world" (John 16:33).

This is why we need the spirit of power. You don't need power if trouble is just an illusion. You need power if you are facing something else that is powerful. If you're going to defeat an army, you need a more powerful army. Fear itself is powerful, so you need more power to overcome it. Fear can be physically, mentally, and emotionally overwhelming. We need a power that is strong enough to push it back, to look it in the face and say "I can."

The kind of power God offers is so strong it actually transcends and works in our weakness. The enemy is powerful; Scripture never denies that. It's just that God-who-is-with-us is more powerful.

Paul spoke of encountering an ongoing attack from a demonic spirit. Instead of removing the attack, God gave him power to overcome it:

> He has said to me, "My grace is sufficient for you, for power [*dunamis*—(miraculous) power, might, strength] is perfected [*teleitai*—to bring to an end, complete, fulfill] in weakness [*astheneia*—weakness, frailty]."
>
> Most gladly, therefore, I will rather boast about my weaknesses, *so that the power of Christ may dwell in me.* Therefore I am well content with weaknesses, with insults, with distresses, with persecutions, with difficulties, for Christ's sake; for when I am weak, then I am strong. (2 Corinthians 12:9-10, NASB)

The point is, we are human and weak and frail. Every single one of us can bring God a legitimate list of reasons why we aren't qualified for whatever he's calling us to do. Paul had a long one: *I'm physically weak, I struggle against sin, I have a horrible past, I make everybody mad, and I'm in a heap of trouble all the time.* But that's totally irrelevant, because the strength doesn't come from us. It's not supposed to come from us. It comes from God, and God enjoys working his power through human "jars of clay."

Mercy's Story: "You will keep in perfect peace all who trust in you, all whose thoughts are fixed on you!" Isaiah 26:3 (NLT)

This verse is very relevant to my life. A couple years back I was in a season of intercession for someone I love very much. I knew she was doing some risky things, but I didn't know that the night before I was flying to visit her she was going out with a group looking for paranormal activity. They called it ghost hunting. I call it demon chasing. And unfortunately for me, they were successful. They stirred up something in the dark realm that decided to attack me, instead of her. I had chosen to "stand in the gap" for her and by doing so was positioned between her and the demons that she was chasing that night. As a result, I thought I was going to die.

I was shaken out of a peaceful sleep by something that I could feel but not see. My heart was racing so fast I could not count my heart rate. It felt like my chest was compressed by a weight that I could not lift, and I could barely breathe. While my upper body felt nailed down, my legs were being lifted off the bed and slammed back down. *That* is when I clued in that this was not a heart attack of physical origin, but a demonic assault.

I tried to pray. I tried to rebuke this thing off me. Initially, nothing changed. I felt like I was going to suffocate or have a heart attack.

Then in my mind's eye, I saw Jesus standing on the end of a long dock. I focused in on his face. Although I still felt pinned, I discovered that as long as I could keep my focus on Jesus's face, the violent physical shaking would stop and I could come into a measure of peace. But if that vision would start to drift from my focus, my legs would slam back on the bed and the panic would set right back in.

This battle went on for about an hour. By the end, I was completely exhausted.

I couldn't change my pricy airline ticket, so I had to travel just hours after the incident. Thankfully, I was traveling with Kim who is my amazing spiritual "big sister," and she all but carried me through the airports. But I will never forget the anxiety that I felt on the flights! What if I was attacked like that again on an airplane? It actually took months after that, and at least half a dozen flights, to not feel like I was on the brink of an anxiety attack. My only antidote was Jesus's face in the front and center of my mind and the promise of Isaiah 26:3.

In every circumstance, it's essential for us to know that we are not without power. We may not be able to control something or change it, but God has given us His Spirit, who is a Spirit of *power*. Even when our human frailty and weakness is genuinely too great for us to overcome, the power of Christ works in us. So we are never without power: in every situation we can connect with the power of God. We are not ever truly powerless.

What's in Your Hand?

Nobody in the Bible more closely encountered and experienced the power of God than Moses. Moses was not a military leader. He was not a skilled speaker. He was not more-than-usually smart or wise. He was not wealthy. He didn't have a close relationship with his parents (he never really knew them) or a good marriage. He was a misfit, too Egyptian for the Hebrews and too Hebrew for the Egyptians, who tried to help his people in a bad situation and ended up accidentally murdering someone and fleeing to the desert, where he spent forty years tending somebody else's sheep.

When God appeared to Moses and called him to go back to Egypt and act as God's mouth and hand for the deliverance of his people, Moses offered him a litany of excuses. *The people won't listen to me. I've been gone for forty years, and I was never really one of them in the first place. I'm a nobody. I stutter.*

God just asked him, "What's in your hand?" Moses checked—he had a stick. God essentially smiled and said, "We can work with that!"

(Thanks to our friend Brandi Swindell for this take on the story!)

The absolutely staggering displays of power that came through Moses and his stick did require that Moses take a lot of risks and exercise a lot of faith. But the power never came from him. When it came down to it, Moses was never anything more than an awkwardly misplaced man with a stutter, a stick, and a burning devotion to God.

That was all God needed.

Walking in the Spirit of Power

All of this sounds great in theory, of course, but we're still going to face countless situations where we do not feel powerful. So how do we tap into the power of God?

This is so obvious it almost goes without saying, but

we're going to say it anyway: *tapping into the power of God starts with receiving and believing the truth that the power of God is there for you.* Joshua and Caleb believed they could take the land because God had said so, and they believed him. They had a lens based in truth, and they saw their circumstances through it. The people of Israel, by contrast, saw their circumstance through a lens of distrust and unbelief.

So if you're going to tap into the power of God, you have to take a Moses step and believe it will be there if you pick up your stick. You probably won't feel full of confidence. You'll probably have to do it scared. But you can fill your mind with truth by meditating on the Word of God, and then you can choose to act on it.

Carolyn's Story: When I was about eleven, a bunch of young hoodlums broke into our house while our family was out grocery shopping. When we got back with a van full of food and small children (I had five younger siblings at the time), the vandals were still in the house.

My parents had the unenviable task of dealing with the facts that all their children were in the front of the house as the thieves ran out the back door, the house had been ransacked down to the kids' piggy banks, and their waterbed had been slashed and was leaking through into the lower floor. It was not a moment to inspire peace in anyone!

Even so, I don't remember anything but calmness from my parents as they handled the situation. They were particularly concerned that we not be frightened. As policemen shone their flashlights around the house into the night, my parents put all the kids to bed in one room, partly to keep us out of the way of the flood, partly so we would be together and less scared.

I remember being quite confused about one thing, though: there was an expectation that I would at least be disturbed by the event. I wasn't. I fully assumed that since God was in charge, he would take care of us. What was there to be scared of? Why was this assumption being made by other people that I would be nervous? Why, for that matter, were my siblings upset? Had everyone forgotten that God was in charge?

My simplistic eleven-year-old mind grappled with the problem, assumed people had momentarily forgotten the fact of God's-in-chargeness, and continued on my happy way, secure in the knowledge that though I was little, God was big.

Faith is not always easy, but it is never complicated. Childlike faith, the kind of belief that just says, "God's in charge; why are we upset?" is surprisingly powerful. Childlike faith never comes from thinking that we, the child, the weak one, have things under control. It always comes from looking to someone else to be powerful in our weakness.

There are three key ways we see to tap into the spirit of *dunamis*—the spirit of "I can because God will." There are probably more, but this chapter should get you started.

1. You Can Pray

In every situation, you can pray. But we have a suggestion that might surprise some readers: *don't launch right into prayer as the first thing you do.*

As author and speaker Graham Cooke says, if the first thing you do is pray (in the sense of asking God to do something) you will pray out of your panic and your fear. Your prayers will be an expression of fear, not of faith.

So *first,* take a moment to get quiet. Pray in another sense: not of petitioning God to act, but of asking him for his perspective. Deliberately recall his promises (like "God has not given us a spirit of fear, but of power.")

In Jesus's model prayer, petition for our needs ("give us this day our daily bread"; "deliver us from evil") follows a grounding in higher perspective: "Our Father in heaven, let your name be honored as holy. Let your kingdom come and your will be done, on earth as it is heaven" (Matthew 6:9-13). Take time to seek out that higher perspective.

Don't just inform God of what you want him to do; find out what he's doing, and then pray in alignment with that. When you do this, it forces you to take time to listen, emotionally invest in the prayer, and partner with God—which means you will actually walk in the spirit of power.

Romans 8:26-27 assures us that prayer is already happening on our behalf:

In the same way the Spirit also joins to help in our weakness, because we do not know what to pray for as we should, but the Spirit Himself intercedes for us with unspoken groanings. And He who searches the hearts knows the Spirit's mind-set, because He intercedes for the saints according to the will of God.

We are still connected to strength even in our moments of greatest weakness. We are backed by, empowered by, and enabled by the Spirit of God.

2. You Can Cast Your Cares

First Peter 5:6-7 urges us to "Humble yourselves, therefore, under the mighty hand of God, so that He may exalt you at the proper time, casting all your care on Him, because He cares about you."

There is so much in this verse! The word "care" is also properly translated "worry, anxiety, concern." In Greek, it comes from a root that means "to divide," indicating that our worries—our anxieties and cares—distract and divide us. This is a powerful picture of fear! Most of us want to please God, to obey him, and to use our talents well. But the natural cares and concerns of life can distract us from our purpose. Anxiety kicks the legs out from under us so that when we want to stand, we fall.

Peter's solution is appropriately Peter-like: it's bold, proactive, and violent. He instructs us to cast our cares on God—literally throw them at God. The wording in Greek doesn't just indicate throwing our concerns away; it indicates throwing them to God, onto his shoulders.

Peter connects this with humility. Basically, in the game of life, don't just stand there holding the football. If you do, the entire field is going to come down on top of you, and you're not big enough to handle it. Hurl that thing at the quarterback and let him take it into the end zone.

The best part of this verse is its reasoning: "Because he cares for you." What you care about, God cares about, because he is committed to taking care of *you*. He has taken responsibility for your responsibilities. You can aggressively throw your anxiety at God and trust him to handle things for you.

Given that anxieties are intangible and so it can be a little hard to figure out how to throw them, we suggest actually doing something physical to mark it out. One of us (Rachel, for the record) once spoke a particular set of anxieties over a rock and hurled it into a pond. It worked.

3. You Can Take Action

In business, you will hear about the need to develop a "bias toward action." Fear is paralyzing, and one of its biggest lies is that you are powerless—so one of the best ways to counter it is to be proactive to whatever extent you can. Stepping out and doing whatever you *can* do can be a great way to walk in the Spirit of power.

In church circles, there can be a tendency to see passivity or fatalism as faith. We will just do nothing so God can do everything. But God very rarely ever called anyone to do nothing. Moses had to pick up his stick. Joshua had to march around Jericho. A life of faith is a partnership with God.

This is seen quite clearly in 2 Timothy, surrounding this very discussion of the spirit of fear versus the spirit of power. If you'll recall, the original context for that verse was Paul's statement that Timothy had been given a gift by God, one fear would try to stop him from using. Like all of us, Timothy had a contribution to make.

In regards to this gift, Paul goes on to write in 2 Timothy 1:12, "I know the One I have believed in and am persuaded that *He is able to guard what has been entrusted to me* until that day." Two verses later, he turns around and gives Timothy an exhortation: "*Guard,* through the Holy Spirit who lives in us, that good thing entrusted to you" (v 14). The words used are exactly the same. Paul tells Timothy in one breath that he can trust God to guard the gift, and in the next breath that he must guard it himself. A partnership with God is in view.

Do you remember the circle of influence from chapter 4? That concept is so powerful because it urges us to be proactive. We need to recognize our ability to influence a situation and then *do it*. We need to develop a bias toward action. It's great to pray for God's help with our finances, our health, or our relationships, but in all of those areas we also need to be proactive to guard and develop the gifts he has given us. In a very practical way, taking action puts you in touch with the power you have in a situation and circumvents fear. What you can do is your responsibility; what you can't is God's. It's empowering to do what you can.

Paul was weak. Moses was weak. Joshua was weak. They all saw the power of God at work in radical ways—not because they didn't recognize their own weakness, but because they knew their weakness was just an invitation for God's power to show up. You need to get out to the edge of what you can do in order to see what God can do.

There's a saying we like: "Faith is jumping off a cliff, knowing that either God will catch you or you will learn to fly." The power of God is there for you. It's your choice to access it or not.

7
Chapter

In the Bible's annals of courage, one story that stands out is that of Esther.

Esther, whose Hebrew name was Hadassah, lived in the time of her people's greatest troubles. As a nation, they had been violently removed from their homeland and forcibly resettled in Babylon. Their cities lay in ruins, and their temple was a pile of rubble.

God's prophets had foretold all this destruction and warned the people to repent of idolatry and apostasy, but they did not, and now there was nothing to do but wait out the exile, cling to their identity and faith, and trust that God would one day restore them to their land.

In Babylon, the captive Israelites enjoyed a measure of favor because of people like Daniel, who served the Babylonian king. But Babylon's days, too, were numbered. The empire fell literally overnight, overrun by the combined might of the Medes and Persians.

That, of course, put the Jewish people in Babylon back to square one. Whatever privilege they had won was lost. They were now just one more captive nation under harsh pagan rulers.

This is the setting of the book of Esther, which opens with a party. In the Persian fortress city of Susa, the Persian king, called in this book Ahasuerus (his historical identity is somewhat open to question), is holding a six-month feast to display "the glorious wealth of his kingdom and the magnificent splendor of his greatness" (Esther 1:4). At the end of this party, Ahasuerus summons his wife, Vashti, in order to show off her beauty. But Vashti is holding a party of her own and refuses to come.

This sets off a firestorm of controversy. The wife of the most powerful man in the world can't refuse to come when he calls—he'll be humiliated, and all the women in the empire will get empowered, resulting in "contempt and fury," according to the wise men (Esther 1:18).

The decision is quick and unanimous: Vashti must

go. She is publicly and promptly deposed. And to under-score how deeply she is being humiliated, a search will begin so that "her royal position is to be given to another woman more worthy than she" (Esther 1:29). The king of course already has a large number of secondary wives and concubines, but the search for this new queen is to be extremely public and far-reaching. It's all part of mak-ing Vashti's downfall spectacular.

What precisely happened to Vashti—and whether we should view her refusal to come and be shown off as a vice or a virtue—is a matter of debate. It's possible she was killed or exiled. More likely, she remained in the king's harem, demoted from queen to ultimate reject.

After a four-year search, a new queen is indeed cho-sen: a young woman named Esther, who happens to be Jewish. The girl is an orphan, raised by her cousin Mor-decai, and he has given her one strong command: "Esther did not reveal her ethnic background or her birthplace, because Mordecai had ordered her not to" (Esther 3:10).

Everything in Esther's life reeks of instability and danger. When you've been chosen to underscore some-body else's rejection, the point cannot possibly be lost on you that you are vulnerable to the same thing. Harems were not safe, happy places; they were backstabbing, competitive communities where everyone vied for favor and poison wasn't unheard of. If a rival king was to take over the throne, the entire harem would be murdered to make sure no unwanted descendants ever cropped up.

Esther's people still lived in the shadow of the horrifying, bloody overthrow of their nation. They were strangers in a strange land. They had seen Babylon overthrown and their own tenuous political position lost. Esther herself had lost both parents, and her father-figure warned her sternly not to let anyone know who she really was.

Esther was young—probably little more than a teenager when she found herself part of the Vashti replacement campaign. Rather than seeing her exaltation to the throne as a position of power, she must have seen every step further into the public eye and the changeable affections of the king as a step further onto a tightrope existence that might snap at any moment.

When you are a mouse, the last thing you want is the eye of every cat in the nation fully fixed on you.

The Wrong Side of the Law

Mordecai, meanwhile, got into the habit of spending time daily at the King's Gate so he could keep an eye on Esther and give her advice when she needed it. As a result, he crossed paths with a member of the king's court named Haman the Agagite. Their meetings were not exactly congenial. Haman's ability to hate and hold grudges proved monumental, and he hatched a plot not only to kill Mordecai, but to annihilate all of his people too. It was the captive Jews' worst nightmare come true.

Haman had quite a bit of favor with the king, and it wasn't hard to convince him to put Haman's plan into action. Esther 3:13 tells us, "Letters were sent by couriers to each of the royal provinces telling the officials to destroy, kill, and annihilate all the Jewish people—young and old, women and children—and plunder their possessions on a single day, the thirteenth day of Adar, the twelfth month."

Esther, living a woman's typical secluded life behind harem curtains, knew nothing about any of this. Her short-lived glory had already dissipated; she hadn't been summoned by the king in a month.

But then Mordecai sent word to her.

Esther responds right away: "All the royal officials and the people of the royal provinces know that one law applies to every man or woman who approaches the king in the inner courtyard and who has not been summoned—the death penalty. Only if the king extends the golden scepter will that person live. I have not been summoned to appear before the king for the last thirty days" (Esther 4:12).

Essentially, Esther's response boiled down to, "I can't go to the king about this any more than you can. If I try, they'll kill me. It's not likely I'll even reach him to talk to him. I have no real power; you know that. I'm only here in the first place because the king wanted to prove he couldn't be wrong."

She was right. But the need was urgent. Mordecai responds with a famous injunction: "Don't think that you will escape the fate of all the Jews because you are in the king's palace. If you keep silent at this time, liberation and deliverance will come to the Jewish people from another place, but you and your father's house will be destroyed. Who knows, perhaps you have come to your royal position for such a time as this" (Esther 4:13).

The implied rebuke in his words is perhaps unwarranted—because Esther immediately steps up, with a plan and more courage than Mordecai gave her credit for.

"Go and assemble all the Jews who can be found in Susa and fast for me. Don't eat or drink for three days, day or night. I and my female servants will also fast in the same way. After that, I will go to the king even if it is against the law. *If I perish, I perish"* (Esther 3:16). We are told that Mordecai "went and did everything that Esther had ordered him."

From that point on, Esther carries herself with a dignity, strength, and cunning that belies her years. She risks her life by *approaching the king*—a Vashti-like show of potential disrespect, but this time with a death penalty attached to it—and then, when he has chosen to respond to her with favor instead of anger, carefully orchestrates events so that Haman outs himself as a villain and the king's fragile ego is never provoked into a dangerous backlash.

It's only when Haman has been killed, Mordecai exalted to his position, and Esther herself revealed as Jewish that she truly lets her heart show. Told that the king's orders can't be reversed, she reveals what has driven her all along. Clearly, it's not been fear for herself:

> Then Esther addressed the king again. She fell at his feet, wept, and begged him to revoke the evil of Haman the Agagite, and his plot he had devised against the Jews . . . "For how could I bear to see the disaster that would come on my people? How could I bear to see the destruction of my relatives?" (Esther 8:3, 6)

The spirit that enabled Esther's extraordinary courage was love. She loved Mordecai, loved her people, and loved her God. Had she only loved her own life, she would have played her cards very differently. An often overlooked piece of this story is that Ahasuerus twice offers Esther anything she asks, up to half his kingdom. Instead of using this as an out to save just her own life, or to gain wealth and power for herself, she continues to push the boundaries by asking him to reverse his own decision, effectively asking him to humble himself and look foolish—something he has deposed queens over before.

Given the opportunity to save herself, Esther doesn't take it. She forges on, determined to save her people, because for her, this whole thing was never really *about* her.

Fear does not drive her in this story. Love does.

Love: The Anti-Fear

Our key verse in this book tells us that instead of the spirit of fear, God has given us the spirit of love. Of the three gifts listed in 2 Timothy 1:7, love has the central place. And for good reason. If you did nothing else that we suggest in this book, but you did focus on growing in love, you would find yourself walking freer and freer of fear almost as a side effect.

Love is the anti-fear. It is a whole worldview, lens, and approach to life that is exactly opposite to fear. Interestingly, love actually accomplishes many things that fear tells us it can accomplish, making fear redundant. Love protects, sets boundaries, and is appropriately jealous. Love creates security and sets our feet on solid ground. Love takes care of us.

> **LOVE ACTUALLY ACCOMPLISHES MANY THINGS THAT FEAR TELLS US IT CAN ACCOMPLISH, MAKING FEAR REDUNDANT.**

When love is in place, fear does not need to be.

Love is a fundamentally different orientation to life than fear. Fear is about ourselves. It's inward-looking, isolationist, protectionist, and scarcity-minded. It filters everything through the questions of "How will this affect me?" and "Is this safe?" Love by contrast is outward-looking, communal, generous, and abundance-minded. It filters everything through the questions of "How will this affect others?" and "Is this good?"

Love shapes our character in a way that is fundamentally different from the way fear shapes it. Love trusts; fear distrusts. Love gives; fear hoards. Love believes; fear will not go out on a limb. Love seeks unity; fear builds walls.

First Corinthians 13, maybe the best known chapter in the Bible (thanks to wedding ceremonies), tells us what love is:

> Love is patient, love is kind.
> Love does not envy,
> is not boastful, is not conceited,
> does not act improperly,
> is not selfish, is not provoked,
> and does not keep a record of wrongs.
> Love finds no joy in unrighteousness
> but rejoices in the truth.
> It bears all things, believes all things,
> hopes all things, endures all things.
> Love never ends.
> (1 Corinthians 13:4-8)

Fear is the opposite of everything love is. *Nothing that is true of love is true of fear, and nothing that is true of fear is true of love.* Love and fear compete for the same space in your soul; both want to shape and direct your life.

Just as fear and God both want the throne, fear and love are in direct competition for the power to shape you. This isn't surprising given that Scripture says "God is love" (1 John 4:8).

Fear is not patient. It is not kind. It does envy—it is scarcity-minded and constantly comparing. It does act improperly, is selfish, and is provoked. It keeps a record of wrongs and bases its willingness to love or trust others on that record. Fear finds joy in unrighteousness because unrighteousness proves fear "right"; it does not rejoice in the truth.

Fear bears nothing, believes nothing, hopes nothing, and endures nothing. And whereas love lasts forever, fear is destructive. It actively tears down.

The easiest way to overcome fear, then, may be to grow in love. As one grows, it will drive out the other.

Where Love Comes From

The themes of love and fear meet up in 1 John 4:7-18, an incredibly rich passage. We've highlighted some of its key ideas:

Dear friends, let us love one another, *because love is from God, and everyone who loves has been born of God and knows God. The one who does not love does not know God, because God is love. God's love was revealed among us in this way: God sent His One and Only Son into the world so that we might live through Him. Love consists in this: not that we loved God, but that He loved us and sent His Son to be the propitiation for our sins. Dear friends, if God loved us in this way, we also must love one another.* No one has ever seen God. *If we love one another, God remains in us and His love is perfected in us.*

This is how we know that we remain in Him and He in us: He has given assurance to us from His Spirit. And we have seen and we testify that the Father has sent His Son as the world's Savior. Whoever confesses that Jesus is the Son of God—God remains in him and he in God. *And we have come to know and to believe the love that God has for us. God is love, and the one who remains in love remains in God, and God remains in him.*

In this, love is perfected with us so that we may have confidence in the day of judgment, for we are as He is in this world. There is no fear in love; instead, perfect love drives out fear, because fear involves punishment. So the one who fears has not reached perfection in love. We love because He first loved us. (1 John 4:7-18)

There are three big ideas in this passage:

• First, God loves us. He loves us first, before we ever love him. In fact, we learn to love by receiving his love for us. God doesn't just love us in some vague, emotional way; he does so actively, through the gift of his Son—even to the point of dying to make reconciliation with us possible. This is how we know what love is. We access this love as we confess Jesus.

• Because God loves us, we need to love one another. The love of God given to us and for us enables us to love others as well—and as love is perfected in us, fear gets driven out.

• When we love one another, the love of God remains in us. The word "remain" is also translated "abide" or "dwell." The big idea is that when we practice love, not only receiving it from God but also giving it to others, we become a hospitable place for the love of God to get comfy and feel at home. God won't love us less if we refuse to practice love, but if we want his love to feel right at home in us, we need to be hospitable!

God's love is abundant and meant to be shared. His heart is not only for unity with us, but that we might be united with one another. John 17 shows the correlation between love and unity, especially in verse 23: "I am in them and you are in me. May they be made completely one, so the world may know you have sent me, and have loved them as you have loved me."

Fear is bent on staying separate, dividing us from others to keep ourselves from getting hurt. Fear puts up walls, where love seeks unity, relationship, and reconciliation. One leads to breakdown; the other leads to wholeness.

When the love of God remains in us and is perfected in us, it drives out fear.

Love Hurts

One of the epidemics of our culture is being afraid of love, afraid to love. We're made for love and deeply desire it, but the fear that we won't be loved back can be paralyzing. It's interesting that the very thing that is supposed to cast out fear—perfected love—is the thing many people fear the most.

This fear doesn't come from nowhere. It usually arises because this has actually happened to us: we have loved, it wasn't returned, and we got hurt. We need to see this for what it is: an extremely effective strategy of the enemy. We become afraid of the very things—love for God and love for others—that would set us free.

We understand. And we can't promise it won't happen to you—or happen again. Honestly? We live in a world of fearful, broken people, so most likely it *will* happen again. Even people who do love you will fail to love you in the way you want them to, in the way they should. It's a mark of our imperfection that none of us love like God does (yet).

But if you just shut down there, you've closed off the pathway to ever finding true freedom in your life. Because without this key of love, this whole thing of overcoming fear won't work. You can't just have power and a sound mind, but not love, and be free of fear. People try to do this, but it does not work. The three have to work in conjunction with each other.

Out of the three, love is the riskiest. It makes us vulnerable. With a sound mind, you're only controlling yourself. You're just disciplining your own thoughts. This is very low risk: you're not going to get hurt by it. You're sowing and reaping, and in this case you have a high level of guarantee on the crop: almost for sure, practicing sound-mindedness is going to produce mental health. Power is likewise not a high-risk gift: having power is always clearly better than not having power.

But love involves other people, so the risk element is much higher. And again, you can't just say, "Well, I love God but not people." The Bible says that makes you a liar. Love just doesn't work like that (1 John 4:20).

The bottom line is that yes, there is risk here, and you will get hurt again. You will have to do the hard work of learning to forgive, to be healed by God, and to be courageous and open in the face of possible rejection. But the fact is there is no freedom from fear if you stay locked down against love. It's like being dehydrated but having a fear of water. The only real option is to overcome your fear.

The order given in 1 John is key: Receive the love of God for you first. Then live it out in love for others. As you do, the love of God will get comfortable in your life—it will dwell or remain with you. It becomes a virtuous cycle, love enabling more love that enables more love.

The fact is, as much as human relationships can hurt, they can also bring incredible blessing, blessing and strength we'll never know if we close ourselves off. And these human relationships will teach us to love God and receive his love to a new degree. We get on-the-ground practice in loving and being loved by loving other people and receiving love from them. These things prepare our hearts to be more hospitable to God's love for us: to receive it and allow it to dwell in us. His love is much greater and deeper than human love, but human love gives us a vocabulary to begin to understand it.

"Love that Remains"

The "love that remains" is an amazing spiritual reality that anyone can experience. It's important to understand that John isn't saying God won't love us if we don't love others. His love was given to us before we ever even loved him back, let alone loved anyone else. His love is unconditional.

But if we want his love to live with us, and we want to live with his love, we need to make room. God loves his enemies, but his love doesn't remain in them. They haven't received it; they don't honor it; it can't dwell in them. God doesn't dwell with them, and they don't dwell with him.

It's the same in human relationships. We can love our enemies, in the sense of blessing them, caring for them, praying for them, even giving to them, but un-less they receive our love and allow it to dwell in them, honoring it and making it at home with them, there is no relationship. This is why boundaries can be in place even where love is present: while we are called to love (*agape*—honor) everyone, not everyone will become a *phileo,* a love-friend.

God has boundaries. He loves us unconditionally, but he won't force his love on us if we aren't willing to receive it, practice it, and remain in it. Like the prodigal son, we can leave God's love—and like the prodigal's older brother, we can follow all the rules but still miss out on the Father's love because we're not willing to ex-tend it others, and so we demonstrate that we haven't really received it at all.

As the Father has loved Me, I have also loved you. Remain in My love. If you keep My commands you will remain in My love, just as I have kept My Father's commands and remain in His love.

I have spoken these things to you so that My joy may be in you and your joy may be complete. This is My command: Love one another as I have loved you. No one has greater love than this, that someone would lay down his life for his friends. You are My friends if you do what I command you. I do not call you slaves anymore, because a slave doesn't know what his master is doing. I have called you friends, because I have made known to you everything I have heard from My Father. You did not choose Me, but I chose you. I appointed you that you should go out and produce fruit and that your fruit should remain, so that whatever you ask the Father in My name, He will give you. This is what I command you: Love one another. (John 15:9-17)

As we obey God by loving each other, we get to enter God's counsel. We become not just his servants but his friends, people he will talk to and share his heart with. We get access—the kind of access that comes with a relationship where both parties remain in each other's love.

Being Perfected in Love

John is clear that love is a process. It's something we grow in, and as we do, fear gets tossed out. He says, in fact, that perfect love casts out fear.

As we were discussing the content for this chapter, we suddenly saw a connection we'd never seen before—

an aha moment that showed us the trajectory of a life shaped by love.

Love begins when we receive God's love for us, and it grows as we extend love to others—to those John calls our "brothers." But perfected love goes even further. *Perfected love is love for our enemies.*

In the Sermon on the Mount, Jesus taught:

> You have heard that it was said, "You shall love your neighbor and hate your enemy." But I say to you, love your enemies, bless those who curse you, do good to those who hate you, and pray for those who spitefully use you and persecute you, that you may be sons of your Father in heaven; for He makes His sun rise on the evil and on the good, and sends rain on the just and on the unjust. For if you love those who love you, what reward have you? Do not even the tax collectors do the same? And if you greet your brethren only, what do you do more than others? Do not even the tax collectors do so? Therefore you shall be perfect, just as your Father in heaven is perfect. (Matthew 5:43-48)

If anything in the world merits genuine fear, it's an enemy. This is not fear of chance or circumstance; an enemy is someone who is genuinely out to get you. When we have reached a point of genuine love for our enemies, we are perfected in love, and fear is gone. There is simply no room for it anymore.

What does this look like, and how does it really work? Remember, we aren't talking about freedom from feelings. If you have real enemies (and the Bible doesn't deny that some of us do—enmity is real), you may still have to deal with feelings of dread or anxiousness where they're concerned. But those feelings don't have to rule your life or your heart, and they don't have to be given free rein. You can walk in a confidence that is greater than this fear.

David is a great example. In several places in the Psalms he expresses confidence in God and asks: "What can mere man do to me?" He asks this question while he's running from Saul, living his life on the run, often hiding out in caves. He knew full well that Saul could put a spear through his head . . . or his heart . . . or his liver . . . you get the idea . . . at any minute. And yet he expressed genuine freedom from fear. Where did that confidence come from?

Although it's not easy, love for enemies is a pretty simple thing. You love your enemies by refusing to hate them back. You love them by choosing to bless them and pray for them. You love them in your actions.

Romans 13:10 says, "Love does no wrong to a neighbor. Love therefore is the fulfilment of the law." Not every relationship will be close. Not even God has a close relationship with everyone, because not everyone chooses to receive his love. The idea is *agape,* honor, not *phileo,* close friendship.

Where the freedom really comes in is actually in relation to God. Remember 1 John 4:17? "In this, love is perfected with us so that we may have confidence in the day of judgment, for we are as He is in this world." When we are free

> WHEN WE ARE FREE FROM CONDEMNATION BEFORE GOD, WE HAVE CONFIDENCE.

from condemnation before God, we have confidence. If you actually hate your enemy, it becomes a sin-and-forgiveness issue: you are actively in sin and are therefore under condemnation. This isn't even all between you and your enemy; you're afraid that God is going to judge you for a legitimate sin in your life.

But if you refuse to hate your enemy and choose to

bless them back, you *acquit yourself* of any guilt. You take God's side in the whole thing; his love remains in you. The fear of judgment is gone, and love is perfected in you.

Overcome Evil with Good

When we live in fear, we are controlled by evil. The shadow of what evil might do, to us or in the world around us, dictates our beliefs and our actions. Love gives us another way to live. It puts us back in the driver's seat, opens us up to the gifts God desires to give, and makes new life and restoration possible.

We see this even where our enemies are concerned: enemies tend to fear each other. If someone is your enemy, they probably fear you to some extent. But because you don't choose to harbor fear toward them, and you are active in blessing them and choosing not to harm them, the fear becomes one-sided. If one day they decide they no longer want to be an enemy, there is the possibility of a wall coming down and something truly new and good coming into place.

Romans 12:21 urges us, "Do not be overcome by evil, but overcome evil with good" (NIV). When it comes to practical pathways, love is the best there is. We can concentrate on growing in love rather than concentrating on overcoming fear. This takes our focus off fear and puts it on love, which means we are less likely to feed fear and develop it. We don't overcome evil by overcoming evil; we "overcome evil with good."

As you grow in love, fear has to go. It's just the way it is.

In fact, nothing we have talked about thus far actually entails focusing on fear. Holiness, fear of God, devotion and loyalty to him, proactive faith and power—all of these are positive, God-focused, love-growing things.

In the end, fear isn't even really worth our attention. It's as we grow in faith and love that fear gets driven out. Esther wasn't able to conquer the plans of a mass murderer by focusing on her fear. She did it by focusing on love—for God and for her people. In prayer and fasting, she welcomed the love of God. That love remained.

We are able to do the same.

8
Chapter

A SOUND MIND

Rachel's Story: It was an absolutely perfect Fourth of July evening in Marina del Rey, a seaside community in Southern California—clear, warm, and beautiful. I'd been invited to accompany a group of friends, first to visit some friends of theirs for a BBQ and hang-out time, then to head for the marina and watch the fireworks. My friends were wonderful people; the BBQ was delicious; our hosts were welcoming and warm. But there was trouble in paradise.

In the living room, someone was watching the movie *Silence of the Lambs*. I wasn't watching—but I couldn't help catching snatches of dialogue and imagery, enough that the movie's vivid portrayals of evil settled into my mind. I did my best to shake it off, but I was disturbed.

As my friend and I left the house to head for the water, the sudden quiet made me aware of just how disturbed I actually was. It isn't too strong to say that a horror fell over me. I was deeply aware that something unclean and tormenting had come into my mind, and it did not want to leave.

Proverbs 4:23 says, "Above all things, guard your heart, for out of it come the wellsprings of life." I try to be careful about what gets into my heart, but in this case it felt like I didn't have a choice. Whatever was happening in my spirit at the moment, I was aware that I needed supernatural deliverance from it. I asked the Lord desperately to remove it . . . and he did. Within minutes, peace had returned to my soul and the images and ideas from the movie had lost their power.

I know that I could reopen the door to the horror I felt that day, but I have very consciously chosen not to. I'm immensely grateful for the Lord's help in that moment—his gift of a sound mind.

We began this book by pointing out that at its most basic, fear is a natural instinct given to us to protect us from harm. Like other natural, "fleshly" instincts, it turns into sin and becomes a serious problem for us when it's given control and gets out of balance.

But because fear is a natural instinct, it comes along with a bunch of natural side effects, some of which can be fun or even addictive. This is one thing when the rush comes in the form of adrenaline from physical activity, like cliff jumping or riding a roller coaster. It's a whole other thing when the rush comes in the mind and heart—when we use fear to entertain ourselves.

The trouble with using the adrenaline rush of fear as entertainment is that you don't have power to turn it back off. What gets into our minds roots in our hearts, and out of the heart flows the rest of life. It's "fun" at first, but it ceases to be fun when you can no longer enter a dark room without your heart racing, or when anxiety becomes a growing problem for you, or when you're dealing with actual demonic oppression because of doors you have opened.

Toxic thoughts—that stuff that gets into us either because we invite it (by watching horror movies, for example) or because of other people (through trauma, a movie that's playing in the other room where you can't completely get away from it, demonic activity in a home)—change our minds and can create overpowering instinctive fears that usually take leave of reality and cause us to see danger where there isn't any. This is truly tormenting fear.

The effect of horror is just one way fear can mess with our minds. Fear alters our perception of reality in many ways, many of them more subtle. This is why the third gift God gives us to displace fear is the gift of a sound, or disciplined, mind.

"We Must Have Looked Like Grasshoppers"

One common way fear changes our perception of reality is through projecting. If you remember, when the ten spies entered the land, they spotted giants. They came back to the nation of Israel and told them, "We looked to ourselves like grasshoppers, *and so we must have seemed to them"* (Numbers 13:33).

Do you see what happened there? The ten spies couldn't read their enemies' minds. They projected their own views of themselves onto the giants and assumed the inhabitants of Canaan saw them as grasshoppers—totally insignificant, weak, and puny.

The fascinating thing is that they were wrong. When the people of Israel finally entered the land *forty years' later,* they sent two spies to the city of Jericho. A local prostitute named Rahab hid them from her own people. Here's what she told them:

> I know that the LORD has given you this land and *that the terror of you has fallen on us, and everyone who lives in the land is panicking because of you.* For we have heard how the LORD dried up the waters of the Red Sea before you when you came out of Egypt, and what you did to Sihon and Og, the two Amorite kings you completely destroyed across the Jordan. *When we heard this, we lost heart, and everyone's courage failed because of you,* for the LORD your God is God in heaven above and on earth below. (Joshua 2:8-11)

The events Rahab referenced here were decades in the past. Yet her people were still afraid of Israel, even panicked by them, because of what they had seen God do! The ten spies could not have been more wrong in their projection. The Canaanites did not see them "as grasshoppers." While the Israelites were busy looking at themselves and projecting their viewpoint onto their enemies, their enemies were looking at God—and they were terrified.

The ten spies' grasshopper complex wasn't reality. The reality was that the inhabitants of the land were afraid of them. But they projected their own fear and created an alternate reality, and that alternate reality won the day. In this way fear can create mental illness: we literally do not see reality when we are controlled by fear. We lose the ability to distinguish between reality and illusion, truth and lies.

Mercy's Story: Proverbs 29:25 says "The fear of man is a snare." In my life, it was the perfect illustration. I felt caught and held by the fear of other people most of my life. I had the heart to reach out to others and make friends, but I felt tied down. I had an antagonistic lens through which I viewed myself, and I assumed other people saw me through that same lens. It was a mental struggle in every social setting.

My self-critical thought pattern went something like this:

I bet they will be distracted by the huge gap between my teeth. I know they can tell this outfit came from Bargain-Mart! They would probably rather be talking to anyone else in the room, and I would just be annoying them.

Many times this stopped me from ever stepping out and starting a conversation. But I was so torn because I genuinely love people and had a deep longing for connection.

Finally, I was convicted of my self-focus and determined to stop negatively obsessing over myself and instead turn my focus to the other person and ask God, "What do they need from You? And how can I be a blessing to them?"

At the time I didn't see myself in a healthier light; I simply chose love over fear. It was the first step toward a long journey out of that fear and into a more solid identity.

Come to find out, most people didn't even share my lens anyway! People often thought I was pretty and even smart. But I never would have discovered that if I wasn't brave enough to step out of the snare of fear.

The Gift of a Sound Mind

The mind is our primary battlefield for spiritual warfare. It's where we access God's gifts and put them into practice—or not. So it's good to know that God himself has given us what we need to win our battles. A "sound mind" is a gift of God.

In English, the idea of "soundness" is something that is solid, firm, and stable. The Greek terms here are also translated "sound judgment," "wise discernment," "prudence," and "discipline." Our minds are designed to operate in a way that aligns with reality: to be solid, stable, wise, and disciplined.

As we've already seen, though, God's gifts need to be received and then proactively put to use. The gift of a sound mind is powerful, but we need to use it.

For example, in a fear situation, we can discipline our thoughts. When our mind starts racing with "what if" scenarios, projections, and trying to predict what's going to happen in the future, we can pull them back to order. We can tell our thoughts, *"No, don't do that. That hasn't happened. You don't know that. Cross that bridge when you come to it. Don't assume the worst."* We can consciously recognize when we are creating an alternate reality, choose to stand on truth instead, and stop the runaway freight train of fear in its tracks.

A sound mind doesn't mean you won't ever get battered by thoughts like these. Fear is always ready with a suggestion, and the enemy loves to jump on board as well! But disciplining your thoughts, while it isn't fun, is powerful—especially over time, as it becomes a habit and the pathways of your thoughts become more and more ingrained in truth and stability.

Everyone can learn to do this. It's like a muscle: the more you use it, the stronger, easier, and more automatic it gets.

Starve Your Second Mind

One of our favorite verses is James 1:8: "A double minded man is unstable in all his ways." We love this verse because we have so much experience with it! As human beings, we tend to entertain "two minds" about most things. We trust God . . . but we also harbor doubt. We think we can probably accomplish that certain thing . . . but we're also keeping a list of reasons why we might not be able to. We know truth, but we keep wavering back and forth.

All of this double-mindedness makes us unstable. It connects us back to 1 Peter 5:7, which we read in the chapter on "Power." There, we read God's invitation to cast our "cares" on him, and we saw that "cares" comes from a root that means to divide or distract.

Worship leader Misty Edwards likes to say that following Jesus isn't hard; it's only hard when we're half-hearted about it. What's hard is being only partially committed. Things get easier when you make the choice to leap—to go all the way.

James earlier said that "he that wavereth is like a wave of the sea driven with the wind and tossed" (James 1:6, KJV). Double-mindedness makes us ineffective in prayer, ineffective in overcoming, ineffective in pretty much everything. It leaves us subject to the wind: whichever way the wind is blowing is where we're going to end up.

We need to make a decision to be of one mind and one mind only. That's why concepts like fear of the Lord, holiness, and love are so powerful in overcoming fear. They direct all our fear to one place, establish our identity as set apart only for God, and give us one way of living. When we are holy, we are whole.

There are two ways to conquer this "two minds" problem. The first is to commit—leap—get all the way in. Stop holding back and make a decision to trust God all the way, no matter what, and no matter how hard you have to fight to support that decision.

The second is just as practical: starve your second mind. When we're double-minded, it's because we're trying to hold to God's Word and also a conflicting view-point of our own. If we spend time building both of these, they're going to come into conflict, and we're going to be unstable in our minds. We need to give God's Word the high place it deserves.

Get Aligned with the Word of God

The best way to practice soundness of mind is to align ourselves with the written words of God in the Bible. The Bible contains words inspired by the same God who spoke our world into existence and sustains it by his word: the truths of Scripture are literally as solid as the ground you're standing on and as secure as the gravity holding your cells together.

As we were writing this book, our pastor, Marc Brule, told the story one Sunday of his battle for peace as a young man. At nineteen, he was faced with the problem of rampant, out-of-control, deeply irrational fear—the kind of fear that is tormenting. It had entered his life in various ways, some of which were under his control and some of which were not.

Marc chose to combat fear by meditating on peace. He looked up every Scripture in the Bible that contained the word "peace" and listed them out—over four hundred of them. He read every single one, chose the ones that were most significant to him, and memorized them. He made a point of going over and over these verses in his mind, even speaking them out loud when fear would begin to rise up in him, and of obeying their directives. He militated against fear by meditating on peace.

What Marc did was work. It took effort, and it took time. But in the long run it paid off: the peace of God began to rule his mind and heart where fear had ruled before.

We get free of fear's control as we do the same: as we learn, read, memorize, and meditate on the Word of God.

As part of a ministry called Restoring the Foundations, our friends Daryl and Lynne Hovey teach on overcoming ungodly beliefs or "UGBs," in our minds. It's not enough just to try to stop ourselves from thinking lies. We need to actually replace those lies with truths given to us in the Word of God. We can't do this without learning what the Word says and intentionally, deliberately building it into our thought lives.

Most of us are familiar with Jesus's promise that "the truth will set you free." But that promise (like most of God's promises) has a condition attached to it: *"If you continue in My word,* you really are My disciples. You will know the truth, and the truth will set you free" (John 8:31-32). Truth will set us free when it becomes a regular, continuous, integrated part of our lives.

Do the Stuff

G.K. Chesterton famously wrote, "The Christian ideal has not been tried and found wanting. It has been found difficult; and left untried." In our knowledge-oriented Western world, this is probably the biggest missing piece in the discipleship puzzle: *it doesn't work if you don't do it.*

In Matthew 7, Jesus described two men, one who built his house on rock and the other who built it on sand. We often equate this with knowing Jesus or not knowing Jesus. But Jesus said both men heard the Word of God. What set the man who built his house on rock apart—and made his home so firm and stable that it stayed standing in the midst of a tremendous storm, while his friend's house collapsed—was that he obeyed what he heard.

As you learn the Word of God, be intentional to put it into practice. You can't build confidence in the Word of God if you never put it to the test. The love of God is transformative, but not if you don't receive it. Forgiveness will set your heart free, but not if you never forgive. Peace will guard your heart and mind, but not if you don't choose to turn your worries over to God.

Once again, a voice from the business world sums it up well: "Insights become effectiveness only through hard systematic work ... The greatest wisdom not applied to action and behavior is meaningless data" (Peter Drucker, *The Effective Executive*).

Applied to the Bible, this means that whenever you see a command, do your best to obey it. When you gain an insight, first measure your current actions against that insight, and then if you need to, adjust the way you're living (thinking, speaking, acting, praying). Ask the Holy Spirit to help you. This is how we walk by the Spirit, and it's how our lives are changed.

Learn in Community

All of this learning and obeying doesn't need to happen in a vacuum. God has given us the community of faith—his people in the body of Christ—so that we can build each other up in knowledge, in practice, in encouragement, in compassion, and in help.

And He personally gave some to be apostles, some prophets, some evangelists, some pastors and teachers, for the training of the saints in the work of ministry, to build up the body of Christ, until we all reach unity in the faith and in the knowledge of God's Son, growing into a mature man with a stature measured by Christ's fullness. *Then we will no longer be little children, tossed by the waves and blown around by every wind of teaching, by human cunning with cleverness in the techniques of deceit.* But speaking the truth in love, let us grow in every way into Him who is the head—Christ. From Him the whole body, fitted and knit together by every supporting ligament, promotes the growth of the body for building up itself in love by the proper working of each individual part. (Ephesians 4:11-16)

The perspectives and fellowship of other people can be tremendously helpful in practicing a sound mind. There are times we just can't get outside our own heads enough to see what we can't see. Others can remind us of truth, widen our lens, and pray for us. In turn, we can do the same for them.

Just watch that you don't bring negativity and fear to the party. Our job is to build each other up, not tear each other down. Ephesians gives great advice here: "Do not let any unwholesome talk come out of your mouths, but only what is helpful for building others up according to their needs, that it may benefit those who listen" (Ephesians 4:29, NIV).

Turn Off Negative Input

As you learn the Word of God, practice it, and participate in healthy community, remember not to feed your "other mind"—watch what's going into your mind, and where you can, turn off negative input. Input that is specifically designed to provoke and build fear is toxic input. You might like it (horror movies, for example), but it's not healthy for you, and you won't be able to control its effects—just like you can't drink a Coke but opt out of the calories.

News can be similarly unhealthy, in that it fills our consciousness with "circle of concern" information delivered in a way that is deliberately designed to keep us afraid and dependent on the newscast. For many people, turning off the news may be a practical first step toward getting free of anxiety.

And yes, you may even need to limit contact with certain people or learn proactive ways to counter their input into your lives. If someone in your life is only pro-voking anxiety and fear in you, it's important to learn how to counter it.

Live Love

We are in a battle, and the mind is the primary bat-tlefield. Thank God, he has equipped us with a sound mind, and we can learn to discipline our thoughts so that we can kick fear to the curb.

Ephesians 6:10-17 sums it up well:

Finally, be strengthened by the Lord and by His vast strength. Put on the full armor of God so that you can stand against the tactics of the Devil. For our battle is not against flesh and blood, but against the rulers, against the authorities, against the world powers of this darkness, against the spiritual forces of evil in the heavens. This is why you must take up the full armor of God, so that you may be able to resist in the evil day, and having prepared everything, to take your stand.

Stand, therefore,
with truth like a belt around your waist,
righteousness like armor on your chest,

and your feet sandaled with readiness

for the gospel of peace.

In every situation take the shield of faith,

and with it you will be able to extinguish

all the flaming arrows of the evil one.

Take the helmet of salvation,

and the sword of the Spirit,

which is God's word.

Paul's exhortation here closes with a less-familiar injunction: "Pray at all times in the Spirit with every prayer and request, and stay alert in this with all perseverance *and intercession for all the saints*" (Ephesians 6:18).

He goes on to ask the Ephesians to pray for him and for his work in the gospel. It's a reminder that although we are in a battle, and the battle is mostly in our minds, the battle isn't about us. We are part of something bigger, and the needs of others matter deeply. We can orient ourselves to the fight out of love and looking outward, not out of fear and looking inward.

If you are living in an alternate reality, this is a great first step toward coming back to the truth. And that is the power of a sound mind.

9
Chapter

WALKING ON WATER

The first time fear ever shows up in the Bible is in Genesis 3, and it's a tragedy. In Genesis 1 and 2, we read how God created the universe by his Word and shaped mankind out of the dust with his own hands. We read the Creator's joyful opinion of the whole thing: "It's good ... it's very good." We read that God gave mankind dominion and walked in fellowship with them in Eden.

But then comes the lie. The decision to doubt, to disbelieve God's goodness. The fall—the choice to "break faith" with God.

Moments later God comes looking for Adam . . . and he's hiding.

Fellowship has been broken. Trust is gone. Love is nowhere to be seen.

It has been replaced by fear.

When God confronts Adam, Adam does not respond with repentance or ask for God's help. Instead, he shifts the blame onto Eve. So right there human relationships fall apart too. Harmony, love, and fellowship give way to shame and blame and hiding.

Ever since then, fear has been telling us that we can't trust God and we can't trust others. Fear has been urging us to hide, to avoid shame at all costs (because surely, we think, shame will be the result if anyone sees us for who we really are), and to believe that life has been created for our harm and not our good.

When God asked Adam why he was hiding, he said, "I realized I was naked, so I hid." It's like Adam had just realized, for the first time, how small and weak and powerless and vulnerable to harm he was. He thought that was why he was hiding. But the reality is, he misdiagnosed the problem. He had always been small and weak and powerless and vulnerable to harm.

What had changed was that before, he was in close relationship with God—and now that relationship was broken. *That* was the change that brought fear into the world.

The Real Reason We Wrote This Book

We wrote this book because we want you to overcome fear. We want fear's control in your life broken so that you can have peace, so that you won't be stopped from investing and multiplying your "talent" in the world, and so that you can experience the freedom and joy of a courageous, powerful, loving, and sound life.

But most of all, we wrote this book because fear stops us from loving and knowing God. *And we want you to love and know God.*

In the garden, the breaking of faith with God broke everything. It shattered human trust and community. It cursed the earth. But most tragically of all, it replaced relationship with God with exile from God's presence. Adam and Eve left, not because God didn't want them anymore, but because they didn't want him. They left the presence of God in their fear and in their shame and in their newfound legalism, their attempts to cover up their own weakness and pretend to be strong on their own, and their descendants began a breathtaking race to the bottom that soon covered the entire world with violence and enmity.

Most of us are still living in that place of fear and shame and legalism. Even people who have been born again still struggle to really know, trust, and love God. We struggle to believe that intimacy with God is possible—that he even wants intimacy with us.

But he does. All of Scripture testifies to that.

That is the biggest reason we want you to overcome fear. We don't just want you to walk on water—*we want you to walk on water to take Jesus's hand.*

Shame, Hiding, and Legalism

Genesis 3:6-10 tells us what happened immediately after the fall:

> So [the woman] took some of its fruit and ate it; she also gave some to her husband, who was with her, and he ate it. Then the eyes of both of them were opened, and they knew they were naked; so they sewed fig leaves together and made loincloths for themselves.
>
> Then the man and his wife heard the sound of the

Lord God walking in the garden at the time of the evening breeze, and they hid themselves from the Lord God among the trees of the garden. So the Lord God called out to the man and said to him, "Where are you?" And he said, "I heard You in the garden *and I was afraid because I was naked, so I hid."*

Adam and Eve were naked, as they had been since the beginning: totally open, vulnerable, and without shame. They were weak, but it didn't matter. But the moment they broke faith with God, they realized their nakedness in a way they hadn't before. They felt shame, and with it, fear. Their response was to try to cover themselves.

We might view this as the first instance of legalism or what some would call "religion": trying to cover up an internal problem by external means. They were trying to use works to prove they were really something. But this is really just another form of hiding. It's a way to avoid being known or seen.

Even today, many of us are running around in the fig leaves of our own religiosity. Even though we know Jesus loves us and died for us, and even though we believe God will save us, when he comes looking for fellowship with us our instinct is to cover up. Fear begins to flash its neon sign: *Danger. Something here will harm you. You are weak, and God will know it and will reject you.* And we respond by trying to hide—often behind our works.

But this kind of behavior is just more of the same thing that sent us away from God's presence in the first place. It's still a lack of trust, a fear of God that isn't good or holy, but is doubting and disbelieving. Fear keeps some of us locked away from God's presence all our lives.

But it doesn't have to be that way. Remember, God came looking for Adam and Eve. And when he came into the world as an infant, Jesus came looking for you. He's still looking for you, and his offer isn't just "salvation someday," it's fellowship now.

When Jesus Comes . . .

Jesus came into the garden of the earth in search of men and women who would answer his call. And the first thing he preached was "Repent": what we didn't do in the garden is still an option. We can be restored; we can turn around.

Jesus followed the call to repent by proclaiming, "For the kingdom of God is here" (Matthew 3:2). Just like fellowship with God, the dominion originally given to Adam and Eve in the garden can be restored; *it's still on offer.*

Of course, answering Jesus's call is risky. If we seek out relationship with God, we'll become vulnerable again. Shame may come into play.

Christian speaker Paul Keith Davis often says that sin doesn't separate us from God; shame does. God has dealt with sin on the cross. Sin does not keep us from God; fear and shame do. We have to make a choice to get past the shame in order to come to him to be cleansed and healed. That is the difference between saints and everyone else.

> ## SIN DOES NOT KEEP US FROM GOD; FEAR AND SHAME DO.

To come to Jesus, we'll have to be brave. We'll have to risk shame. We'll have to embrace our own weakness and quit pretending to be more than we are.

But we can do it knowing that we are not alone. In one of Scripture's most breathtaking pictures, Jesus too was naked—but he didn't hide. He hung naked on a cross for a crowd of mockers to see, totally open, totally vulnerable. He wasn't immune to shame . . . but for him, the hope of restoration with us far outweighed it. Hebrews 12:2 says that Jesus "for the joy that lay before Him endured a cross *and despised the shame and* has sat down at the right hand of God's throne."

First John 4:16 says, "And we have come *to know* and to believe the love that God has for us. God is love, and the one who remains in love remains in God, and God remains in him." The Greek word translated "know" is *ginosko,* which indicates a personal, first-hand, experiential knowing. And it goes both ways: 1 Corinthians 8:3 tells us that "those who love God are known by him."

This isn't head knowledge, just the knowing of information. It's intimacy and love.

Jesus gave up everything for intimacy with us. Many will never really enter. Many of us settle for surface knowledge, head knowledge, herd knowledge. The tree of knowledge is still with us, and it's still competing with the tree of life. We can enter into intimate relationship with God; it's really up to us. We all have the same access. How we use that access is our choice.

So what do we do if we're not there? If we know

about God but we don't really know him—not the way we're talking about here, not the way we want to?

The answer couldn't be simpler: we just repent.

Repentance Is for Saved People Too

We sometimes think of repenting as something only the unsaved need to do. If we are Christians, our thinking goes, we repented sometime in the past and we don't need to do it again unless we sin badly.

Actually, repenting is something we can do all the time. It's a course correction. The Greek word translated "repent," *metanoeo,* most literally means "to think differently afterward." It emphasizes a change of *mind* or of thinking that leads to a change of living, in particular a change that happens at a certain point so that afterward, everything is different. One scholar calls it "a cosmic shift of mind and heart."

Whenever we discover that fear is keeping us from God, we can repent. When we find ourselves covering up with legalistic behavior, we can repent. When we put our trust in our own strength instead of our connection with God, we can shift and put our trust back where it belongs. When we entertain a toxic thought, we can repent and build a new thought, a healthy one. When we realize we're letting fear direct our decisions, we can repent and give love back the reins.

On their website, the Greek Orthodox Archdiocese of America describes repentance this way:

> Repentance is not to be confused with mere remorse, with a self-regarding feeling of being sorry for a wrong done. It is not a state but a stage, a beginning. Rather, it is an invitation to new life, an opening up of new horizons, the gaining of a new vision.
>
> The Greek term for repentance, *metanoia*, denotes a change of mind, a reorientation, a fundamental transformation of outlook, of man's vision of the world and of himself, and a new way of loving others and God.

A Cycle of Repentance

As Christians, we live in a cycle of action, repentance, and new action. Remember Peter walking on the water: fear and God are vying for the same thing. Peter couldn't keep a simultaneous focus on both God and the circumstances. We try to do this a lot: we want to keep our eyes on all the problems and then add a pious "But God is in control!" Our focus on the circumstances means our piety doesn't take us very far. Fear takes charge, and we lose connection with God.

But the answer is simple repentance, course correction. We take our eyes off Jesus and put them on our circumstances, we sink. We put our eyes back on Jesus, he pulls us back up, and we're immediately restored to fellowship with him. It's a continual process of renewal and reorientation.

The whole process feels risky, and it's embarrassing how often we sink. But we can tell you this from experience: the more times you go through the cycle, the more you get to know the faithful heart of Jesus—experientially, for yourself. Take the risk. Despise the shame.

Walking on water is worth it.

Proactive Relationship

Jesus calls us to repent and receive a kingdom. This means we have to take responsibility for ourselves in a massive way. We can't repent without accepting responsibility for our past beliefs and behaviors. We then receive dominion or authority in the kingdom of God, which means again that we have responsibility: we're given a talent (or two or five or ten), we're called to holiness, we're placed into relationship with God.

That means even though the kingdom is a gift, we're not supposed to be passive about it. Right from the start, receiving the kingdom means we're accepting that we can and must act. We realize that this is necessary in the rest of life—in parenting, in education, in our careers—but we can get so stuck on the "surrender" and "release control" parts of our faith that we forget God has given us things to do, too. And what wonderful things!

Get proactive and intentional about your relationship with God. Be proactive and intentional about your own spiritual growth. God will bless you in this pursuit, but you must pursue. Don't just sit there and wait for God to drop the Holy Spirit on your head and transform your life. You have a part in this.

Take Not Your Holy Spirit from Me

Mercy talks about a progression in her life where she went from being afraid of God as a child, to being angry with God as a teenager, to coming to a place where she realized how desperately she needed to cling to God. When the biggest fear in her life became the fear of being *without* God, everything changed for her.

David, Israel's greatest king, shared a similar feeling in Psalm 51. This is David's "comeback" psalm, his psalm of repentance after his terrible fall into sin with Bath-sheba. In this beautiful, heart-wrenching plea for cleansing and forgiveness, David writes, "Do not banish me from Your presence or take Your Holy Spirit from me."

What we love about this is the clear truth that even through David's worst sin, God didn't remove his Holy Spirit from him—but David had experienced a wakeup call. He realized that the Holy Spirit could be removed; he could end up without God. That scared him more than anything. It was a holy fear, and it led to a renewed hunger and thirst for God.

When we think of people in the Bible who hungered for and clung to God, David stands out. His life is a monument to overcoming fear. He stood on faith that he would be king while he was being hounded and hunted by Saul. He wrote the words "The LORD is my shepherd, I shall not want," probably during his youth tending sheep himself. He lived the truth of the words, "Though I walk through the valley of the shadow of death, I will fear no evil."

David is one of our favorites because he so ardently sought and hungered for God. We want to know the same kind of spirit-and-body "panting" David described, a desire for God so deep it's like being thirsty in a desert.

Throughout his life, David encountered God in powerful ways. But we don't actually have stories about David dramatically encountering the presence of God the way Moses or Joshua did. What we do have is a record of David spending a lot of time alone in nature, meditating on the Word of God (his laws and promises), and spending time in prayer and in worship. David sought intimacy with God in ways that are accessible to all of us. He was proactive in the simple things, and that crafted his life into one of profound revelation and love for God.

What David did is not out of reach for anyone. You are not disqualified from intimate relationship with God if you haven't had visions and visitations and miraculous encounters. David had the Word of God; he loved and treasured and meditated in it. This is within all of our grasp.

God relates to us as individuals, and every individual relates differently to God. This is part of the point—he wants a close relationship with you and me. Although patterns do appear in the way God relates to people in the Bible, there is also dramatic differences. Peter and John and Paul—these men are the "super apostles," but they all relate to God very differently, based on their own gifts and strengths and personalities. (John, incidentally, uses the *ginosko* concept twice as much as anyone else in the New Testament; this was his lens—personal love.)

This brings us back to the parable of the talents. It wasn't about comparing what you had to what somebody else had. It was about using what you had to the fullest. Paul says comparison is "not wise" (2 Corinthians 10:12).

We have all been given the invitation to come into intimate relationship with God. We can choose to set aside our "fig leaves" and come fully into the presence of God, allowing him to know us as we are so that we can know him as he is. We can stop trying to be something and let him be everything. He will give us our true identity back (you really *are* something, just not through your works and efforts). He promises to cleanse us, forgive us, love us, and make us new.

> **THIS BRINGS US BACK TO THE PARABLE OF THE TALENTS. IT WASN'T ABOUT COMPARING WHAT YOU HAD TO WHAT SOMEBODY ELSE HAD. IT WAS ABOUT USING WHAT YOU HAD TO THE FULLEST.**

Coming to God in this way can feel like the scariest thing there is—but it is the most important reason to overcome fear.

Love Is the Great Reversal

In the garden of Eden, trust was broken, leading to fear, shame, and shattered relationships. The relationship of love that God call us into reverses the whole process. We receive love from God and then give it to others, rebuilding trust, faith, fellowship, and harmony. In Jesus, we can come back to the garden.

We pray that you will.

We'll leave you with a few final words from David:

The LORD is my light and my salvation—
whom should I fear?
The LORD is the stronghold of my life—
of whom should I be afraid?

I have asked one thing from the LORD;
it is what I desire:
to dwell in the house of the LORD
all the days of my life,
gazing on the beauty of the LORD

and seeking Him in His temple.

My heart says this about You,
"You are to seek My face."
LORD, I will seek Your face.

I am certain that I will see the LORD's goodness
in the land of the living.

Wait for the LORD;
be strong and courageous.
Wait for the LORD.
(Psalm 27:1, 4, 8, 13-14)

10
Chapter

THE POWER OF A FEARLESS LIFE

In the pages of this book, we've covered a lot of ground and introduced you to a lot of heroes: people who lived courageous, world-changing lives. From Joshua, the man without fear; to Esther, the woman who dared an empire's disapproval; to Peter, who came back from soul-shattering failure to lead the church through tumultuous days.

They were real people, just like us, but in hindsight they can be a little intimidating. We aren't military commanders and queens and apostles. We're just ordinary people trying to find our courage.

We get it. So we want to introduce you to one more person from the Bible before we close this book. His name is Gideon.

Gideon was neither self-confident nor seemingly brave. He needed a lot of reassurance. He was afraid of his food being stolen. He was afraid of the Midianites. He questioned God. He asked for signs—a lot of signs. When he realized that he had seen the Lord, he was afraid he was going to die. He was afraid of his dad and family. He was afraid of the townspeople. Not to say his fears were irrational. Gideon had real reasons to watch his back. The point is, he was afraid. But God patiently coached him through his fear, and he used Gideon powerfully.

He can and will do the same for you, if you're willing to go the journey.

Who, Me?

You've probably caught on by now, but if not, let us be transparent about what we're trying to do here: from the start of this book, we've been trying to change the way you see yourself. We've been trying to open your eyes to the value you bring to the world, the call upon your life to be consecrated wholly to God, and the love

God has for you. These truths are the reason to over-come fear, the reason to "do it afraid."

It's all worth it, because God's purposes for you are more significant than you can imagine.

Gideon was a man with a high calling on his life. He lived in ancient Israel before the era of the kings be-gan, during a time when God mediated his rule through his chosen judges and deliverers. During this period, Is-rael frequently rebelled against God, and whenever they did, they became vulnerable to the enemies. In Gideon's lifetime, the enemy was Midian, a powerful neighbor-ing tribe that regularly raided and terrorized the Israelite people.

The situation was pretty bad:

The Israelites did what was evil in the sight of the LORD. So the LORD handed them over to Midian seven years, and they oppressed Israel. Because of Midian, the Israelites made hiding places for themselves in the mountains, caves, and strongholds. Whenever the Is-raelites planted crops, the Midianites, Amalekites, and the Qedemites came and attacked them. They encamped against them and destroyed the produce of the land, even as far as Gaza. They left nothing for

Israel to eat, as well as no sheep, ox or donkey. For the
Midianites came with their cattle and their tents like
a great swarm of locusts. They and their camels were
without number, and they entered the land to waste
it. So Israel became poverty-stricken because of Midian, and the Israelites cried out to the LORD. (Judges
6:1-6)

God responded right away. He had a plan to deliver Israel from Midian, and that plan was a man named
Gideon. We meet him just a little later, in verses 11 and
12. The Angel of the LORD (aka God himself in human
form) appears to Gideon and greets him: "The LORD is
with you, mighty warrior."

Sounds good, right? A mighty warrior is just what
they need. But there are two problems with this. First,
when we meet him, Gideon is threshing wheat in a
winepress. He's hiding. And second, Gideon responds to
the angel's greeting with a mouthful of doubt. His immediate response is to question the angel's declaration that
the Lord is with them at all:

Gideon said to Him, "Please Sir, if the LORD is with
us, why has all this happened? And where are all His
wonders that our fathers told us about? They said,

'Hasn't the LORD brought us out of Egypt?' But now the LORD has abandoned us and handed us over to Midian." (Judges 6:13)

The Lord's response is to ignore Gideon's protests. He simply says, "Go in the strength you have and deliver Israel from the power of Midian. Am I not sending you?" (verse 14). Gideon jumps on this statement too: not only is he fairly convinced the Lord is not with them, but he is sure he doesn't have any strength. His family, he tells the angel, is "the weakest" in their tribe, and he himself is "the youngest" in his family. No strength. The Lord must have the wrong guy.

The angel answers with what, by now, should be a very familiar answer. Gideon's weakness is irrelevant. His circumstances are irrelevant. Even his freaking out is irrelevant. For one reason:

"But I will be with you," the LORD *said to him.* "You will strike Midian down as if it were one man." (Judges 6:16)

The Lord Will Be with You

That one truth is the foundation of a fearless life. Just as the Lord was with Gideon—and with Joshua, Moses, David, Esther, Peter, Paul, Timothy, John, and the rest—so he will be with you. In fact, the Lord's promise to you is deeper and more profound than his promise to be with Gideon. Because you live in the New Covenant era, God promises to place his Spirit inside of you, to dwell with you forever and "seal" your future irrevocably, if you place your faith in him.

> For every one of God's promises is "Yes" in Him. Therefore, the "Amen" is also spoken through Him by us for God's glory. Now it is God who strengthens us, with you, in Christ and has anointed us. He has also sealed us and given us the Spirit as a down payment in our hearts. (2 Corinthians 1:20-22)

Fear will do everything it can to stop you from realizing God's promises. It will try to surround your life with walls that keep you shut down and shut in, with your talents buried and your view of yourself limited to "I am nothing but a grasshopper, and everyone else must know it." It will create an alternate reality and wear you out with cares and the exhaustion that is a divided mind.

But you don't have to let it. You can live free from fear's control, free from its dominance, because you are set apart for God, and the Lord is with you.

The Power of a Fearless Life

Through the pages of this book, we've looked at nine facets of overcoming fear.

1 YOU HAVE A GIFT, AND IT IS IMMENSELY VALU-ABLE. *You* have been given something of immense value. In fact, *you are* of immense value. Crafted into your personality, your gifts, your affinities, and your skills is something of huge value, plus the ability to multiply it. Even if you have received the least of all possible gifts, it is still the spiritual equivalent of a million dollars! Fear is a thief and will try to prevent you from ever stepping up to realize the fullness of what God has given you. To counter this, God has given us the spirit of power, love, and a sound mind. It isn't about getting free from feelings, but about overcoming the control of fear in your life.

2 FEAR AND GOD ARE COMPETING FOR THE SAME PLACE IN YOUR LIFE. They both want lordship. It's counterintuitive, but the best way to make sure fear does not rule our lives is to cultivate a special kind of fear: what the Bible calls "the fear of the Lord." This is the one truly appropriate and healthy fear, and it sets you free from fear of anything and everything else. Joshua was almost completely free of natural fear because he walked in such a high level of the fear of the Lord. This fear is a matter of deep honor, see-

ing how big God is and how small we are, and respecting and trembling before the "wildness" of God's being. This is the fear that is love. *The basis for freedom from fear is not that nothing bad can happen, but that the Lord is with us.*

3 FEAR ISN'T NEUTRAL. IT MANIFESTS. It may manifest as arbitrary walls we build around our lives—walls that have nothing to do with reality and yet will shape our identity and cage our effectiveness. You can take back the ground of your inner life. Receive dominion and authority from God and stake your claim: from now on, this ground belongs to Yahweh. Everything that comes in or out has to go through the door, which is Jesus. The giants must fall, high things must be torn down, and weeds must be pulled up. Finally, get busy planting the ground with new seeds: seeds that will give you a kingdom harvest. In the same way that Joshua took physical ground, we are called to take back the ground of our minds, thoughts, and emotions.

4 CONTROL IS A COUNTERFEIT FOR DOMINION THAT WILL KEEP US IN FEAR. We never truly have control, though we do sometimes have the perception of it. When it comes to taking dominion, the only thing we can legitimately control is our own reactions and decisions. We are the limit of our own dominion. When we step beyond that limitation, trusting in our ability to control rather than

in God, we are vulnerable to the dominance of fear. *Our fearlessness must be based not on our own power in a situation but on God's.* This allows us to embrace process and live a truly surrendered life. We need to be about obedience, not outcomes.

5 TO BE HOLY AS GOD IS HOLY IS TO BE SET APART, consecrated, and devoted to God and for God. It is to be marked as specially his, and in that way to be set apart and made different from everyone else in the world. Though holiness is sometimes viewed askew as a list of legalistic rules, it is actually a liberator from guilt resulting in fear. It turns ordinary Christians into giant-takers. Holiness gives us the strength to stand alone, as everyone must do at some point in their lives. Counterintuitively, this also allows us to engage in healthy community as we move away from herd instincts to a community of mutual contribution and accountability. Holiness changes our fundamental self-concept: we are not here for ourselves, but for God. We don't belong to ourselves, but to God. Everything in our lives is for God and through God.

6 OFTEN, WE FEEL AFRAID BECAUSE WE FEEL POWERLESS. GOD SAYS THE OPPOSITE. He says we are strong; we are able. We have the power of the Holy Spirit, the dynamite strength of Christ. To quote Paul, "I can do all things through Christ who strengthens me" (Philippians

4:13, NKJV). If you're going to tap into the power of God, you have to take a Moses step and believe God's power will be there if you pick up your stick. You probably won't feel full of confidence. You'll probably have to do it scared. But you can fill your mind with truth by meditating on the Word of God, and then you can choose to act on it. Our power is not in ourselves but in the fact that God is with us. The spirit of power is the spirit of "I can because God will."

7 LOVE IS A FUNDAMENTALLY DIFFERENT ORIEN-TATION TO LIFE THAN FEAR, and it shapes our character in a way that is fundamentally different from the way fear shapes it. Fear is about ourselves. It's inward-looking, isolationist, protectionist, and scarcity-minded. It filters everything through the questions of "How will this affect me?" and "Is this safe?" Love by contrast is outward-looking, communal, generous, and abundance-minded. It filters everything through the questions of "How will this affect others?" and "Is this good?"

8 FEAR CREATES AN ALTERNATE REALITY in which we lose the ability to distinguish between reality and illusion, truth and lies. God gives us the power to discipline our minds, see truth, and align with reality. We can tap into the power of a sound mind by cutting off or limiting negative input, by meditating in the Word of God, and by practicing

truth. Truth will set us free when it becomes a regular, continuous, integrated part of our lives. God has given us community as well, where we can tap into the power of accountability, perspective, and love.

9 GOD IS CALLING US OUT OF FEAR AND SHAME TO KNOW HIM IN A PERSONAL AND INTIMATE WAY. We are called to a proactive walk with God in which we seek him, build up our faith, and engage with his love and presence in our lives. This is the ultimate reason and reward for overcoming fear. God has begun a great reversal of what happened in Eden because he wants intimate relationship with each one of us.

10 THE BIGGEST REASON TO OVERCOME FEAR IS TO RETURN TO INTIMATE FELLOWSHIP WITH GOD. Fear stops us from loving and knowing God. Jesus's coming began "the great reversal," where everything lost in Eden can be restored. Even people who have been born again still struggle to really know, trust, and love God. We struggle to believe that intimacy with God is possible—that he even wants intimacy with us. But he does. We can proactively seek the presence of God, as David did, course-correcting as we go by repenting and aligning our minds with truth. God wants an authentic, intimate, and personal relationship with each one of us.

Fearless in His Love

Gideon's story does not end with him embracing the call on his life and riding forward in victory, with never another doubt. In fact, right after the Angel of the Lord tells him that his weakness is irrelevant because God will be with him, Gideon says, "Okay, look, wait here while I go and prepare a sacrifice. If you're still here when I get back, I'll know all this is real."

We're not sure if Gideon thought he was hallucinating or if he was just hoping God would go away, but when Gideon came back with his sacrifice and the Angel was still there, his response was literally to cry out, "Oh no, LORD God! I *have* seen the Angel of the Lord face to face!" (Judges 6:22).

If Joshua went into the promised land with a drawn sword and a brave heart, Gideon delivered the same land with what we can only call a chicken spirit. He did it afraid. He asked for a sign—and then another sign—and then another sign. When God told him to begin by tearing down his father's idols, he did it at night, because he was too scared to be seen.

Ironically, when Gideon finally did gather an army, God told him to let everyone who was afraid leave. Gideon probably wanted to be the first one to go home!

In the long run, though, Gideon obeyed. He was scared every step of the way. But we don't remember Gideon as a coward. We remember him as a hero. He won a miraculous victory over the Midianites, because he did it through the presence and the power of the Lord.

He was just obedient. God took care of the outcome.

And his story shows us something else: that God is okay with process, that he loves us in our weakness, that if we're willing to step out on the journey, he will prove to be endlessly patient. The same God who reached out and caught a sinking Peter by the hand coached and helped Gideon every step of the way.

The night of their victory, before they had put their plan into action, the Lord spoke to Gideon:

> That night the LORD said to him, "Get up and go into the camp, for I have given it into your hand. *But if you are afraid to go to the camp,* go with Purah your servant. Listen to what they say, and then you will be strengthened to go." (Judges 8:9-11)

Gideon was afraid. So he went with his servant, and together they overheard their enemies talking about a supernatural dream they had just had, in which Gideon and his army defeated them. The enemy soldiers themselves proclaimed, "This is nothing less than the sword of Gideon son of Joash, the Israelite. God has handed the entire Midianite camp over to him."

That night, the Israelite army won a tremendous victory. They shouted out a battle cry: "The sword of the LORD *and Gideon.*"

Whether you're already out on the battlefield or still hiding in the winepress, God is calling you, Mighty Warrior, to overcome fear. He will be with you all the way. When you're afraid, he'll help you.

If you're willing to do it afraid, you will overcome. The victory is guaranteed, because the Lord is with you.